TWELVE
SMOOTH
STONES

CHUCK MEYER

TWELVE SMOOTH STONES

A father writes to
his daughter about
money, sex,
spirituality, and
other things
that really matter

Northstone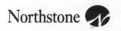

Editors: Michael Schwartzentruber,
Dianne Greenslade
Cover and interior design: Margaret Kyle
Consulting art director: Robert MacDonald

Credits
Front cover photo:
Photography West, Kelowna, BC, Canada,
Wayne Duchart MPA

Author photo:
Grant • Guerrero Photography, Austin, Texas

Northstone Publishing
acknowledges the
financial support of the
Government of Canada
through the Book
Publishing Industry
Development Program for
its publishing activities.

Northstone Publishing is
an imprint of Wood Lake
Books Inc., an employee-
owned company, and is
committed to caring for
the environment and all
creation. Northstone
recycles, reuses, and
composts, and encourages
readers to do the same.
Resources are printed on
recycled paper and more
environmentally friendly
groundwood papers
(newsprint), whenever
possible. The trees used
are replaced through
donations to the Scoutrees
for Canada program. Ten
percent of all profit is
donated to charitable
organizations.

**Canadian Cataloguing in
Publication Data**
Meyer, Charles, 1947–
           Twelve Smooth Stones

ISBN 1-896836-27-5

1. Teenage girls–Conduct of life. 2.
Teenage girls–Religious life. 3. Parent
and teenager. I. Title.
HQ798.M49 1999   248.8'33
C98-911111-3

Published by Northstone Publishing,
an imprint of Wood Lake Books, Inc.
Kelowna, British Columbia, Canada

Printing 10 9 8 7 6 5 4 3 2 1

Printed in Canada by
Transcontinental Printing

for Michal
with love and gratitude

Contents

FOREWORD

I am Michal, just a normal teenage girl. I have an active social life and I like to party. I am no exotic beauty nor an important scholar. I have made no contributions to science and I have done nothing beneficial for humankind. I have no claim to fame. To the outside world, I am just another in the sea of the nameless and faceless. I am, however, special to my family and friends who know and love me. That is all that matters.

I admit that it is exciting and embarrassing to have not only a few stories, but an entire book about me for everyone to read.

I do not think it extraordinary that I have a good relationship with my parents, because most of my friends also seem to have good relationships with their parents. What infuriates me are the people who willingly stereotype all teenagers based upon what they have seen on TV or read in newspapers. It is true that some teenagers engage in law-breaking acts, but the operative word is *some*. No one has the right to classify all teenagers as rebellious, drug- and alcohol-using lawbreakers.

I believe that this book shows the medium range. I am not extremely rebellious, but I *do* fight with my parents and they *do* constantly annoy me. We have our arguments and differences (I am always right), but we are usually able to work out a compromise that benefits everyone so that we can live happily and peacefully.

I enjoy having a good relationship with my parents. I am not saying that if someone does not get along with their parents they are horrible people. It is understandable when parents and children disagree. Getting along with parents may not make anyone's life better and a good relationship does not necessarily make anyone a better person. But I am most free when I consent to listen to my parents. When I live in accordance with their rules I find that they happily award me with more respect, trust, and freedom.

Although I don't tell my parents everything that goes on in my life – only my friends hear *everything* – I do tell them *some* things. I feel better knowing that if I were ever in a bad situation they would know enough to be able to help me out and to understand my predicament. I also know that my parents respect and trust me enough to allow me to do whatever I want, within reason. They were teenagers once and they know more than I do about *some* aspects of the world. Often I find that acknowledging their advice and experience benefits me. I do not have to be rebellious to do what I want to do. I am happy that I have the option to choose to run my life the way that I want to.

This is a book about my many experiences, and about my dad's perception of them. I think that many people around my age, 17, will relate to these stories because similar events have occurred in their own lives. If that is true, I hope that these letters will help.

INTRODUCTION

I first met Michal when she was six and I was 39. I was sitting on the porch with her mother, Debi, whom I had recently met and was getting to know better. In the middle of a conversation we were distracted by the splashing sounds of what could only have been a medium-sized porpoise in a bathtub behind us in the house.

"What is that?" I asked, hoping beyond hope it was a dog or a small calf and not a child that would confound, entangle, and otherwise obstruct any plans I might develop with this wonderful blue-eyed woman.

"That's Michal."

Oh great, I thought dejectedly, it's a boy. A kid was bad enough. A boy kid was a deal breaker. There was no way I could even think of raising a boy kid, having been one myself and knowing the possibilities. In my mind I was out of there.

"She's ready to come out of her bath."

Hmmm. A girl kid. Named Michal. I hesitated, imagining myself in the car, driving home. Fast.

Debi stood and invited me in for a cold drink. I walked inside and waited in the kitchen while she went to dry the kid.

"What's he look like, Mommy?" came the little duck voice from down the hall. "Is he cute?"

"Go see for yourself," her Mom wisely said.

Suddenly I was confronted with the sight of a giggling six-year-old with dark wet hair dripping on a fluffy bath towel that was twice her size.

She stared. I stared back. What do you say to a six-year-old?

Nervously I broke the silence. "I'm Chuck, who are you?"

"Michal," she squealed, as she turned and ran down the hall, her little hiney sticking out of the towel. Mooned by a midget.

I wondered what in the world I was getting into as I hollered around the corner to her Mom: "Thought we might go for some ice cream if you want."

"Great! Be ready in a minute," she answered.

Not to be left out, Michal yelled, "Wait for me-mer!"

I did wait. And the nickname "Meemer" stuck.

That was more than 10 years ago and Michal is now 17. She is in the National Honor Society, is a "volleyball stud" with a slam that imprints the word MIKASA on the forehead of whoever is unlucky enough to try to block the ball. She has a wonderful sense of humor that sneaks up on me and makes me laugh despite myself, and she has her mother's unusual combination of assertiveness, independence, beauty, and common sense.

My first interactions with her were compiled as a part of *God's Laughter And Other Heresies*, in which she taught me the lessons of elementary school. Our preadolescent, junior high years together are logged in *Fast, Funny, And Forty*. But as full-blown adolescence approached, newer, different issues arose on the horizon. Incidents occurred that caused me to reflect more deeply than was possible in a ten-minute discussion (sometimes argument) or a snide sound bite that leapt from my mouth before I could censor it. I wrote my reactions to the incidents and left them in Michal's "in-box" – the wooden box in my office where I put her mail or messages so she can grab them as she passes through in a blur. She would read them eventually and sometimes comment or sometimes not, as the mood moved her. Sometimes they would result in my absolute favorite thing with her – when she would wander into my office and initiate a discussion that would lead down a labyrinth of ideas and insights about everything from psychology to war to college to evolution.

Occasionally I let friends read what I had said and they would comment on their own similar interactions with their own teenagers. I asked their kids to read them as well. Reactions were positive, but the most surprising thing was that the parent and child spent time chatting about the issue. Sometimes the chatting was arguing, sometimes listening, sometimes short, sometimes longer. But they took each other seriously, even if only for a nanosecond, and that bit of time cannot be undone. Maybe next time it will be two nanoseconds. In any case, my hope in publishing these pieces is that parents might find another way to succeed at their purpose of protecting and loving their kids and that teenagers might find a way of relating to adults, including parents, that results in growth rather than resistance.

I was on an airplane with a guy one time, a complete stranger, and we were discussing kids. Michal was about 11 and I was prematurely lamenting the onset of adolescence. The man, not much older than I, disagreed. He indicated that the studies done in the 1940s on which our stereotype of the horrors of adolescence are based were all conducted with sociopathic and dysfunctional kids. So the stereotype is neither true, nor required. In fact, he argued (and I have seen recent studies to support this), *normal* adolescence is characterized by relatively good relationships between parents and kids.

It drives me stark raving nuts when some idiot TV newscaster pontificates his or her opinion that "This story shows the majority of teens

_____." Fill in the blank. Usually it's "are into sex, drugs, and rebellion." Or "smoke, drink, and do drugs." Or "love alternative rock, rap, and gangsta." Or "hate their parents, won't go to school, and get into trouble." The fact is the *majority of teens* are out there being responsible, friendly, caring, and contributing members of society. They are in school, working, volunteering, trying their darnedest to figure out what in the world is going on inside and around them, being bombarded by adults with mixed messages and by peers with demands for fun. Most kids get along with parents (at least as often as the parents get along with each other) and while mood swings and independence are certainly major issues, they need not result in hatred, resentment, or permanent estrangement.

Of course things are not always rosy with kids, but they are not always rosy at work or with spouses or family either. Even when kids do their best, and even when parents do their best, the worst can and does sometimes happen. But to *expect* that adolescence will be especially difficult conveys overtly or subliminally to the child that this is our presumption about how he or she will be – and they will fulfill this self-fulfilling prophecy if we set it up for them.

My expectation with Michal has always been that she will be a great adolescent because she is a great kid, a good person. I not only love her, I *like* her a lot – for who she *is*, not for who I can make her into. The older she gets the better she gets, the more available she is for conversation, for independent thinking that challenges me sometimes and, at other times, affirms the conclusions to which I have come. As you'll see from the following pages, this does not mean we don't have differences of opinion, sometimes vociferous. But for some reason we both hate it when that happens and, after a cooling-off period, we usually work it out, often with a sense of humor about it.

As long as I've known her, Michal has had a box in her room where she displays little treasures she's picked up on her way through life thus far. There are seashells, an arrowhead, a tiny pine cone, a couple of buttons, and some carefully chosen, well-worn stones from various locations. When she looks at these objects, I would guess that she is reminded of where they came from, and that memory may serve to comfort her, to affirm her, to warn her, or to empower her. It is my fondest wish that these *Twelve Smooth Stones* would serve the same purpose, that she will look upon them and draw what she needs from them, when she needs it.

The title also has another reference. When Michal was little, Debi's favorite song to sing to her was *Only A Boy Named David*, which told the story of David and Goliath. The biblical account is significant. When young David was going out to engage the giant Philistine, David's father, Saul, "clothed David with his armor; he put a helmet of bronze on his head, and clothed him with a coat of mail. And David girded his sword over his armor, and he tried in vain to go, for he was not used to them. And David put them off. Then he chose *five smooth stones* from the brook, and put them in his shepherd's bag...and he drew near to the Philistine" (1 Samuel 17:38–40).

As Michal goes out to engage the world of high school, college, grad school, job, and relationships, the Philistines of choice, cultural conformity, greed, loss, and success will tower over her, threatening her body and soul, seemingly invincible to all around. The traditional adult armor of experience is bulky, unfamiliar, and therefore useless in her defense. So instead of *five smooth stones from the brook*, she has here *twelve smooth stones in a book*, a greater number because I am concerned about the many giant issues with which she will have to contend.

I have no clue where or how she'll end up – either tomorrow or ten years from now. I suspect that, given her personality and attributes and track record, she'll be happy and successful whatever she does and that the way will be strewn with stunned giants. In any case, I know that her journey will be interesting and thought-provoking and I hope she'll continue to let me be a part of it – as she is letting you be a part of it right now.

No matter how old Michal gets, I'll continue to offer her similar stones that have been smoothed by my experience, both difficulties and successes, until, in my older years, she offers some of hers to me.

one

PARACHUTE

For the four billionth time you nearly got out of the house without a quarter. You tried to argue that you had a 20-dollar bill and that's a *lot* of quarters, but I cleverly responded that it was tough to get that $20 to work in a pay phone – and worse on short notice. You grinned and shook your head and took a quarter, telling yourself you would never need it, could never imagine a situation where you would need it, and Dad was being grossly overprotective for a mere trip with Allison to the movies where I would even drop you off and pick you up.

Maybe so. Even probably so.

But what if I wasn't? What if, God forbid, you get mugged in front of the theatre, purse stolen, wallet gone – left with nothing but that little quarter in your shoe? What if aliens abduct Allison and leave you stranded? What if you get sick or lost or just plain want to come home?

The lesson is this: *Always have your own parachute.*

No matter what the situation, do not expect that anyone else will be looking out for your best interests, or your interests at all. Whether you go to a dance, a movie, out to a party, get in a car with friends, go shopping, or to dinner with Mom and me – it is important to think what you would do if it all fell apart. What if the car breaks down, friends get drunk, drugs appear, people do things you don't want to participate in, you feel threatened or sick or uncertain for your safety? You cannot assume that friends will look after you, think about your well-being, or care about your reputation or the consequences of their behavior on your life and future.

So in every situation it is important to remember that you are the master of yourself (and *only* yourself). Even if the situation is falling apart, you don't have to. You can say yes or no and back up those decisions with the quarter by acting quickly and getting yourself out of the situation at the drop of a coin – which will bring one of us adults to whisk you out of there to safety.

Let me be clear about this. This is not about trust. I trust you implicitly. I trust your ability to assess situations for safety. I trust you to stay out of things in the first place that are not conducive to your health, safety, or reputation. You always have. You always make reasonable, responsible, smart decisions when push comes to shove – that's just who you are. All I want to do is make certain you have the *means* to act on those smart decisions – the quarter to back them up, the mouse hole in the locked room, the parachute out as the car or party or date or friend goes sour or gets into dangerous territory.

This is an important lesson for later in life as well. No matter where I am or what decisions I've made, I always arrange to have a parachute somewhere, a mouse hole I can dive for if the situation gets unhealthy. It may be as simple as a quarter in the shoe, or turning around and walking away. It may be as complex as a parachute clause in a business contract, or Plan B in the back of my head if I get fired or some ethical issue arises that I cannot tolerate or support.

Now this does not mean welshing on deals. (You will recall that I was furious when a car dealer did that after we shook on a deal. In Texas that's grounds for hanging.) Nor does it mean backing out of commitments on a whim or merely for personal convenience. Deals and agreements and commitments are to be kept and taken with the utmost seriousness – unless the deal suddenly changes and your safety or the safety of others demands doing the right thing: bailing out, going home, getting rescued by Dad.

But there is a difference between breaking a commitment and appropriately responding to an emergency or an unexpected occurrence that may jeopardize your safety or compromise your beliefs. Most of the time these are pretty clear and you are really good at knowing what to do, pulling the rip cord, calling 9-1-1. But there will be times when you're not sure whether to bail or stay, especially if your friends are pressuring you to take a risk, do something dangerous, illegal, or immoral. How will you know what to do?

Meem, the best I can tell you is to trust your feelings. If you get into territory where you start to feel uncomfortable, or the voice in your head is saying "Watch out!" even if you don't know exactly why – *trust it*. Every time I have ignored that voice I've gotten clobbered. When I listen and follow, things work out better. I wish I could be more specific, offer a rule that always works, but I can't. I'd like to say, "When in doubt, parachute out." That is probably the safest rule of thumb, and there is a lot to be said for it. The shadow of a doubt may be the indicator light on the dashboard of your brain, warning you that something is malfunctioning and you'd better go. If you bail, use the quarter and get dadded out of the situation, you buy time to talk and decide what to do in the future, time that you may otherwise lose recuperating in a hospital or detox ward or jail. But there are some risks you have to take to test your wings; risks involving writing, sports, jobs, friendships, and (okay, I'll admit it) dating. Just remember, no matter how far into something you get, the parachute cord is always an option.

Now I know that this is not the place to really get into either of the following issues, but you know how compulsive I am in not wanting to leave any stone unturned or any opportunity for you to say, *"You never told me about that!"* So, just for the record, you will hear people say that marriage and pregnancy are two commitments that should never be bailed on. Come see me if you ever need to parachute on either and we'll chat. There's no easy answer to those two, except to say that people make mistakes, forgiveness is possible, relationships die ("till death do us part"), and while abortion ought not to be used merely as a form of birth control, it should be a choice available along with others. This does not mean that marriage and pregnancy ought to be easy to get out of; maybe they should be harder to get into, and should not be entered into with the thought of getting out. Such decisions should be made with counseling, mediation, sadness, grace, and forgiveness.

So keep that quarter in your shoe, or in the little coin purse I gave you for just such a purpose (though it has probably been eaten by the crack behind your bed by now). As you get older and technology gets better, I'll replace the quarter with a cell phone or whatever new thing is on the market allowing instant access like in *Star Trek*. (Maybe by then I can simply "beam" you up and out.) And when I'm not around to back up that quarter, I trust you'll find someone else to catch you when you need to jump.

two

FUNDAMENTALISTS

You just returned from the annual church ski trip exhausted and ecstatic about the great time you had, your increased skills, the encounters with boys, and an obviously enhanced sense of independence and confidence. The only real bummer was an encounter with some Fundamentalists – those "leaders" from the church who told you that Tarot cards, horoscopes and psychics were things of the devil, and that, since Jesus was the only way to get to heaven, Jews, Buddhists, and Hindus were out.

First of all, let me congratulate you on maintaining your cool. You shook your head in disagreement, spoke up for your Jewish friends and Eastern religion relatives (not to mention common theological sense) and even though their comments offended you and made you angry, you simply left to go do something important, like comb your hair. Good job, girl. I hope you can maintain that same sense of surety and unwillingness to stay around insanity the rest of your life.

I agree with your theological openness – your belief that God can work through any religious tradition God wants to (and even through some things that aren't traditionally "religious"). Why *can't* a Buddhist, Hindu, Jew, Confucian, Taoist, Muslim, Zoroastrian, or totem worshipper who keeps their nose clean, doesn't kill people, acts morally, gives something back to the community and isn't selfish with possessions, get into heaven? Of course they can.

An even better question might be – Why would any group of people believe that *their* way (Jesus or Mohammed or Buddha or Whoever) is the *only* way? Since you asked, I believe the answer is insecurity. Think about it. You'd have to be pretty insecure, uncertain, and worried about who God is to be so defensive and adamant about your specific view of God. What is it they're defending? Why is it so important that they convince *you* that there is only *one* way to see God and it's *their* way? Maybe if they can get you to believe it, it will convince them that they really are right.

If people were *really* secure in their belief about God, they wouldn't be threatened by someone else's view. This is especially true if you believe that God can act through anything God wants to, at any time, any place, and through any person or event. If you believe this, you're on the lookout for God popping out darned-near anywhere, or maybe God's on the lookout for *you* all the time, trying to get a word in edgewise between all the other things clamoring for your attention like TV and clothes and boys and volleyball and youth group and camp and school. In either case, people who are secure about their view of God – or who are willing to be open to God continuing to show Godself to them in new and evolving ways – tend to welcome dialogue about God's existence, embrace different dimensions of God's revelations, and not persecute others who differ from them.

Now – there is a corollary to this. You will find Fundamentalists everywhere, not just in church. There are political Fundamentalists who believe their view of the way to run the country is the *only* one and who are hell-bent on convincing you they're right. My humble experience is that most of them *are* on the "right," but fairness demands that I point out to you there are plenty on the left as well. In some ways those on the left are more seductive because you'd like to believe them and they sound more reasonable – until they get on their soapbox and try to convince you (just like the right-wingers) that their way is the *only* way.

There are other kinds of Fundamentalists as well. Social Fundamentalists believe in either the survival of the fittest (substitute: *rich*), or that all people are equal and require equal opportunity (which must be mandated by law) to succeed. Educational Fundamentalists believe either that people must be rigidly taught or that they naturally learn from their environment in their own way. Sexual Fundamentalists believe either that all sexual thoughts and feelings are by nature unclean and perverse and should be avoided and felt guilty about until you are ready for sex at age 35, or that sexual thoughts and feelings are simply another powerful way to experience yourself and others and have no problem with sex at age 12, with anybody, as long as you use a condom. National Fundamentalists believe the United States is the only nation on earth that is right about everything, or wrong about everything, depending on which end they're on. Health Fundamentalists believe herbs and acupuncture can cure everything, or that only doctors know it all.

The clue to Fundamentalists everywhere is something called (this is a biggie) "absolutizing the relative." This has nothing to do with Uncle Bud or Aunt Kay. It means taking something "relative" like one belief system among many to choose from, and making it the *only* acceptable belief system. It would be like taking one color from the spectrum (say green) and demanding that it is the *only* acceptable color. I believe people do this out of fear of blue, or orange, or red or yellow, which, to me, makes no sense at all. Why is green any more right than purple? Some physicists believe there are 25 dimensions (not just the traditional three or four) so how can people defend one as carrying the truth over the others?

One more comment on the church people who told you you had to take the conservative, difficult but morally superior "narrow road," as opposed to the liberal, morally decaying "wide road" which is paved with parties, sex, drugs, beer, sex, alcohol, tattoos, sex, body piercing, sex, becoming a homeless bag lady leeching out of society undeserved welfare for your fatherless dependent children and, in case I forgot it, sex.

Well (surprise) I see it the other way around. I think the "narrow road" is *much* easier to follow than the "wide road" because you don't have to *think* to stay on it. You just put on your Fundamentalist blinders (whether religious, political, social, or whatever) and keep trudging ahead like a horse or a mule or a slave. You already *have* all the answers, so you don't have to ask questions or fumble for answers to the tough questions like what should we do or who should we be? Worst of all, everyone *not* on your same path is either an enemy or an idiot; they must be converted, convinced, or (worst case Nazi scenario) eliminated.

The "wide road" is much tougher. With no blinders you see *everything* and have to make tough choices that determine your future at every step. Your beliefs are constantly being challenged by forces of *both* good and evil (often disguised as each other). You are forced to *engage* people and circumstances in *dialogue* (rather than the monologue of Fundamentalists) in ways that may be dangerous and risky and have serious consequences for you and your loved ones and your society.

Whichever road you choose (or any combination) I'll do my best to assist. Though I am certainly no self-proclaimed expert, I enjoy the ride – fundamentally speaking, of course.

three

DATE

You had your first real date last night and we all lived through it. Mom and I lost sleep for two nights and got emotionally labile (ready to lose it at a moment's notice) in anticipation of the event – our little daughter was launching out into the unknown (or worse, *known* to us) world of dating. I held firm on my belief that there is a quantum maturational leap between your 14 and his 16 and therefore you couldn't ride in the car with him, even on this double date with your best friend Katy.

It was somewhat reassuring that you knew the boy from church youth group and the church ski trip, though I still would wish for you the experience of dating someone your own age through high school. The grade interests and age differences are just too great to be sustainable over time. But, as you said, "you gotta start somewhere." And my guess is that you will probably always be attracted to older men. You are emotionally mature beyond your years as it is now and that will only increase with experience and age.

Last night Katy came over and you got dressed together; Mom and I drove you (in the *cool* car in case they saw us) to meet them at the restaurant. Walking up to greet the boys, I went first and allowed as how you were lucky I wasn't your Undercover Uncle Bud with a jacket bulge you would have to explain and scare the kid off permanently.

I was glad – but not totally surprised, knowing you – to see they were both clean-cut, sharp-looking kids. While that is no guarantee of anything, it made my stereotypes feel much better. We handed you off to your date, but not before you smooched us goodbye. It was a very tender moment for Mom and me, as though all three of us acknowledged that something was ending and something else beginning. Like kissing us goodbye with permanence.

Mom and I went to a totally edge-of-your-seat distracting movie so we didn't have to think for the next two hours, then came home. I found myself doing little tasks, checking my watch, counting minutes until you would be home and we could hear about the evening, learning that parents are as much involved with the date as the child who goes out on it. You may think you're out there on your own, but if you turn around you'll see that the other guy in the back seat is me.

It's hard for a dad who loves his kid to watch her step over the nest and try out those wings. I know you'll fly fine and that there's nothing more I can do – that the values and guidelines you have in your head are the ones that will guide you from here on out – but that doesn't prevent me from wanting to make sure you don't get hurt by some of the things I know from experience are very likely to be out there.

I remember my first date, Jeannie. I was anxious about it for a week, couldn't eat, major excitement, and, as you can imagine, major kidding from my parents. Jeannie and I were supposed to meet each other at the Cincinnati Gardens skating rink – and couldn't find each other. We both felt awful about it the next day at school, but we remained friends.

A few years later I had a second date, Roxanne, where my brother drove us to a school dance. That she never went out with me again was due to my brother's comments about her that I found immensely funny and she did not. He also found it humorous to flash the bright lights and honk the horn when I was going for the "good night kiss on the front porch routine." I was greatly relieved when I got my driver's license and didn't have to depend on my parents or brother.

I assume it must be a Federal Requirement in some "Guidelines for Parents of Teenagers" book that adults are legally obligated to ridicule their kids' interest in dating, but I refuse. I have told you I will never do anything (intentionally) to embarrass you and I mean it. I remember dating to be a dangerously difficult emotional minefield of anxiety, insecurity, and feelings of hope and failure, not to mention big-time zits that wait exactly one hour before the date to magically erupt, making it appear that you are, in fact, growing another nose. You've got enough to worry about and be excited about without judgmental comments from an adult that make you feel more inexperienced than you already are.

Now this does not mean that I will remain silent. I do have a right to ask, remind, and check stuff: Do you have that quarter in your shoe? Where are you going? Remember your curfew. Call if your plans change. Did the guy remember to bring his report card, birth certificate, and driver's license to show us? Did he correctly complete the Application to Date My Daughter? Did you mention to him what your mysterious Uncle Bud does for a living, and that we don't really know, but that he could suddenly appear at the car door at a moment's notice like The Shadow?

Little things like that are important, and evoke from you one of my favorite sounds: "Daaaaaaaaaaaaaaaaaadddd!" With a grin.

I first went steady with a girl named Rita and that ended badly when I broke up with her at a friend's suggestion – a big mistake in three ways. One, I trusted my friend rather than listen to Rita, not realizing that he may have had other motives.

Two, I didn't have nearly the maturity I have seen you display. When you had a problem with a guy recently, you took the initiative, sat him down and talked about it, asking his perspective and explaining yours – exactly what I should have done but didn't. Three, I should have asked for some adult's perspective, but for a bunch of reasons, good or bad, I didn't. This is something else you do exceptionally well, and I like listening to you talk about your life experience and your questions about it. A big issue with parents and teens is privacy. Parents often want to invade it and kids defend it. I hope you know that I respect your privacy precisely because you are willing and eager to discuss your choices so openly.

The rest of my high school dating career varied from the serious (I thought) to the ridiculous (in retrospect). I usually dated one girl at a time, but not always. "Playing the field" was encouraged back then as a way not to get "too serious." (They thought if you didn't date anyone more than a couple of times nobody would end up pregnant.) As you know, the one girl I kept going back to is the one I eventually married after dating other people in college.

What just occurred to me now is that I don't remember ever once thinking that dating, especially in high school, was a process of practicing social skills and learning to handle new feelings and thoughts and interactions with which I would have to deal the rest of my life. If I had approached it from that angle – from the view of practice – then maybe I would have had a better time at it.

But for some reason I thought of it as "finding someone" in the semi-permanent sense of *having* ("owning") someone to go to dances with, socialize with, go to movies with, and talk with on the phone. You will think this is really dumb/nerdy/immature, but why didn't I know they wouldn't last, that each one was a temporary relationship that would run its course from excitement to boredom in varying lengths of time and be broken off by one of us? Wasn't I paying attention? Didn't I realize after the third or fourth semi-steady relationship that this was the pattern (and the norm) for learning how to relate to the opposite sex? I did not. And I wouldn't have believed anyone who told me that, either. It was serious business, this owning and being owned by someone, which we called dating. In this, too, you are already more mature than I was at your age. You described breaking up with someone as "totally obsessing about him then dropping everything and on to the next one." You are wise beyond my years.

I know you might think this is a parental ploy, but truthfully, the best relationships I had in high school were with "friends." You met Arnold who was my best male friend. We still call each other and talk as personally as we did 40 years ago. I had two major girl friends, people I could ask out and we'd skip the dance and sit and talk for four hours over soft drinks and potato chips, usually at the girl's house, sometimes with her parents.

One was Denni. We helped each other through the traumas and relationships of high school with never a romantic word passed between us. She was like a sister and I'll always be grateful for her. The other was the best combination of friend and romance I had known, Debby Whisenhunt, about whom you know. When she died after our 13 years of marriage, I went back to the dating scene again but this time thinking that no relationship was permanent (more like the attitude I probably should have had in high school). It wasn't until I met your mom (coincidentally a Debi) that I was lucky enough to find again that highly unusual combination of best friend and romance. Okay, okay, okay – and with a wonderful, cute, darling, smart, pretty, bouncy, sensitive, direct, emotionally open daughter in the bargain. (Did I get my lines right?)

So what do I hope for you? I hope you'll keep that incredibly level-headed, down-to-earth attitude that has gotten you through everything so far. I hope that you'll maintain a balance (as you do well) of romance and reality, bouncing from one to the other for all the fun it's worth. I hope that you'll enjoy dating more than I did, be more relaxed about it than I was, see it in the perspective that I didn't, and have a good time practicing social skills that will only increase and deepen with experience. And I hope you'll choose to make the same decisions I did regarding sex and substances, as those were definitely something I somehow had the good sense to do right. ("Right" means healthy, out of trouble, and not hurting anyone else.)

Nice to see you launched on this endeavor, and nice to see that this first run turned out great for everybody. He was a good guy, the movie was fun, hand-holding was exciting, and you were actually seen by a group of popular girls who will be blabbing about you and Katy all next week. Great beginning.

On subsequent outings (he has already asked you to the Junior Prom) I will be constantly vigilant on the other end of the cell phone or pager – just in case you need the parachute. Given who you are and the kinds of choices you make I doubt that need will ever arise. But it makes me feel good as a dad being there. And it gives me something to do until you get home.

four

SUCCESS

"You're really successful, Dad," you said as we rounded the corner to our street. Quite a compliment coming from you, Meem. I thanked you and basked in the specious warmth of your adolescent adoration the rest of the way home. But then I got to worrying about what success looked like from the passenger seat of the car. So I thought I'd better explain the reality of that success, lest you think getting there was easy.

Then I realized that would be perpetuating a lie. Because, in fact, it *is* easy. Or at least easier than most people who are successful will admit. The idea that it's hard is a contamination of the experiences people like Grandma and Grandpa had during the Depression and World War II. Living through the Great Depression, standing in bread lines, subsisting on little or no work and relying on the government for food and shelter, having your dignity stripped by a lousy economy, suppressing your pride to do menial work so you and your kids will eat one more day – *that's* hard. Fighting the Axis powers with everything you've got and trying not to believe the early reports of concentration camp atrocities, rationing food and gas and rubber and aluminum and anything else that can be used in the war effort, living for years without your husband because he's gone to fight, and having to get a job yourself while FDR pulls you out of the Depression and wins the war – *that's* hard.

The generation who lived through all of that survived by gut-wrenching determination and literally heroic effort. People like Grandma and Grandpa refused to give up, continued to help others by sacrificially sharing whatever food and money they had to get friends and family through it as they got through it themselves. Then they slowly, with a lot of hard work and effort, gradually rebuilt their lives from nothing and accumulated an incredible amount of security. They have been enormously successful and their dedication and purposefulness, backed by long hours of often painstaking labor, has paid off dramatically for them.

The problem here is that they think the hardships they endured in the Depression and World War II are *directly responsible* for their successful lives. They think success requires hard work and will tell you so at every opportunity, blaming you (and me) for not knowing "the value of a dollar" and having an easy life with everything given to you.

But equating extremely hard work under harsh circumstances with success must sound very defeating to an adolescent. You already work hard at school and sports and have some idea of the effort that involves. To imagine that you will succeed – make money and be comfortable – *only* by exerting that much and more must sound totally overwhelming given where you are and what your tired, hungry, growing, changing body is doing. So let me offer another version of the truth.

I believe it is relatively *easy* to be successful, but first you have to know what success is for you; you have to define your terms. For most adolescents, success has to do with a combination of popularity and wealth, having all the money you can spend along with a socially glamorous high-profile life. It is often equated with freedom from parental interference, being able to do what you want when you want for as long as you want with whomever you want. Fantasies include skiing the entire season in Winter Park with Brad Pitt and Leonardo DiCaprio; flying off first class to tour Europe and staying in the most expensive hotels with chauffeured cars to take you every place you want to go; driving a red Mustang convertible anywhere.

You will note that neither school nor work is prominent in any of these ideas, possibly because they are so confining, rigid, and irrelevant to the really important things in life – looking good and having money. Exactly where that money comes from is a deep celestial mystery, just as it is on most TV shows, soaps, and every MTV series like *Road Rules* and *Real Life* (which I cynically refer to in my dutiful parental way as *UnReal*

Life because nobody has, like, Real Jobs).

It may be a surprise to you that the same fantasy continues beyond adolescence throughout every phase of life. That's why people buy lottery tickets – on the assumption that if they win the lottery they will be successful, meaning able to purchase anything they want and not ever having to work again. So, indeed, one definition is that SUCCESS = MONEY and vice versa.

My definition of success is *Doing What I Enjoy And Being Paid Well For It.* When young people see older people succeeding it may seem as though those people always knew what they were good at and always got paid well for it. Not true. It usually takes time to figure out what we love doing and how to get paid well for it. It takes time because there are many seductive distractions along the road, like billboards pulling you off in other directions.

Society, through advertising and media, tells you what you *should* want and *should* be good at. According to them, you should want a slim perfect body, a red Mustang, and a hunk of a guy fawning over you, macho-ly. Only then will you be sexy, rich, successful, happy, desirable, and acceptable. And loveable. So a lot of people spend their years going after what they've been told they should want and trying to live up to what they should be. Ultimately these people end up unhappy, depressed, resentful, and unfulfilled. And sometimes dead or in jail.

Part of your task for the next six years of school and work is to explore different things to find out where you fit, what your gifts are, what you are good at and like to do. You may have less-than-desirable jobs to provide the money to allow you to explore what you really want. Or you may be lucky enough to find jobs in a field that you want to know more about and get experience in that before deciding it is or isn't for you.

In any case, there are several things you need to know about success before launching out, or that I need to tell you to fully discharge my parental responsibility. Here they are – in writing.

Other's shoulders

There is no such thing as a "self-made person." Every successful person became successful by standing on someone else's shoulders. We all had help; we all started at the bottom of the heap and took a hand up. We are indebted to the hundreds of people who took time to teach us, show us how to do things, encourage us, open doors of opportunity for us, and boot us in the butt when we needed it. Now of course you have to have the courage to put your hand out and climb up on those shoulders, shaky as they may seem; and you have to take their criticism along with their praise, because you grow from both. And you have to keep searching for people and situations that can best teach you, train you, hone your skills, and help you do what you love to do even better. Find and learn from the masters. Apprentice yourself to them. Learn from their successes and mistakes. Challenge their every move so they can also learn from your youthful perspective – a perspective that they may have lost. I had such people in college, at the pen, at the hospital, and in friendships who modeled the values, attitudes, and wisdom I stand on now.

It is right ("and a good and joyful thing") to be thankful for those who have helped us. Remember the best way to honor them is to do the same for others who will some day stand on your shoulders. Some already do.

The Babe Ruth rule

Not the candy bar, the baseball player. Everybody praises Babe Ruth for hitting the most home runs. Wow. Great record. Incredible. What talent. What power. What success. But people forget how he did it.

He did it by swinging at the ball, and swinging at the ball, and swinging at the ball. He didn't swing a couple of times, get discouraged and quit. In fact, while everyone knows Ruth held the lifetime record for the most home runs – they forget he still holds the lifetime record *for the most times struck out*.

It's easy to see the books and articles I have successfully published, but you need to balance that against my overflowing files of reject slips I've gotten over the years. I got published precisely because I struck out so many times. But if you judged me by adding up totals, I'd have far more numbers in the reject category than in the published category. The measure of success is whether I keep on writing and submitting.

To use your sport of volleyball – success would mean you have a bunch of net balls in addition to some pretty spectacular slams. Both are signs of successful people.

You have already learned about this area. You hustle for the ball, leap, dive, and go for it more than anyone. You have incredible tenacity, staying power, ability to bounce back and keep on bumping. You're doing it in soccer, too, and you do it consistently (and successfully) in academics. You've already learned that there is great payoff in this strategy. You keep going back, discouraged or not, successful or not, and that quality of yours will ultimately carry you into the spotlight of success. You have learned that it is in fact easier on your psyche to persist than to quit, and feels much, much better.

Some people would say this is, in fact, "hard work." I would argue it is commitment to a goal and a willingness to do what it takes, repeatedly, to get there, including striking out.

The Joneses
These are the ones everybody is always trying to keep up with, as though somebody outside yourself sets the standard for you to compete against. In fact, you are your own standard and

the best one to measure yourself by. That's why I like running and writing. I'm competing against myself.

Not to say that there aren't others out there I emulate. I'd like to be as successful with movies as Grisham, as good a writer as Steinbeck, as metaphoric as Tom Robbins, as playful in movie scripting as Spielberg. But I don't want to *be* them. I want to be as good at what I do as they are at what they do. I take it back. I want to be better.

You know what your highest standards are and whether or not you're meeting them. If there's doubt, ask someone who knows you well and who will be honest with you.

Keeping up with the Joneses (or the people who are popular, or get 36,000 on their SATs, or have a car, a big house, and a zillion CDs) usually involves being envious of them, as if they have something you don't. Not true. As Mom is fond of saying, we are richer in love than anyone.

I wouldn't trade places with anybody else on earth. Because the other problem with keeping up with the Joneses is that all we see is their external accumulations. Under that shallow glitzy surface is often unhappiness, fear, abuse, or despair. I have no desire to keep up with that.

90 percent of life is showing up

This is, in fact, a major part of the secret to success. Show up at school and work. Show up whether you want to or not, whether it's raining or hot, whether your car breaks down or you're having a bad hair day. Show up.

This is the easiest part of success and yet the part most people find hardest for some reason. It is incredibly easy to get to work every day with a smile on my face (eventually – when I see friends and colleagues). When people see you doing your job and enjoying it they naturally assume you are doing it diligently and well. That behavior – doing your job without complaining and even asking for more responsibility – leads to promotions and more success. Again, you already do this. You show up at school with your homework done. You show up at practice and do your best – and it has paid off both places.

The other easy part of showing up is treating others fairly – just as you'd like to be treated. People (like you) with excellent verbal and social skills, who are careful and caring listeners and who go out of their way to be helpful, rise to the top. Supervisors like to promote and reward employees who are easy to work with, responsible in their duties, have a good sense of humor, and exhibit their reliability by consistently showing up and volunteering to help out when extra help is needed. Think of people like Ben Welmaker, Sally Heinze, Sandi Aitken, Larry Bugen, Jack Campbell, Ann Richards.

Go the extra ten feet

Roman citizens were required by law to carry a Roman soldier's pack one mile if asked. So Jesus told his disciples to "go the extra mile" and to carry it *two* miles for them as a sign of benevolence.

While that principle is an honorable one and the subject for another letter I am sure, the truth is that in school or work you don't have to do a *whole* lot more than the next person to look and be spectacular. Most people try to figure out the minimal amount they have to do to get by. Quite frankly, that has always seemed incredibly stupid to me. Anybody can be mediocre.

When given an assignment or task, I have always tried to do two things: 1. make it fun for myself by doing something unusual or creative with it and 2. make my boss's job easier. Even if the unusual thing is not really great, it shows you put extra thought into it and tried harder than the next person who did only the amount necessary to get by. In college we were required to list references and footnotes at the back of papers. I heard a professor complain once that it was a pain to have to flip back to the last page every time to check a reference, so I made a duplicate of those pages so he could lay them beside the text and check them more easily. This took little effort (making one extra copy) and yet was perceived by professors as thoughtful and time-saving. Which it was.

Likewise, it takes very little effort to get to work ten minutes early so I can organize my day, get my coffee, rev up the computer, get the lay of the land (and thus a head start) before anyone else arrives, and be seated at my desk ready to take calls when that second hand sweeps past eight o'clock. I leave later than required, volunteer for extra work to take a load off someone else, or suggest something to my boss that might make his/her job easier, in addition to mine.

You usually won't find yourself going a second *mile*, but an extra ten feet often makes the difference between a promotion and getting passed over. In addition, you feel better about yourself and you find people are willing to help you out when you need it. It is especially easy if you like your job and the people you work with.

Now, Mom wanted me to say that you have to be careful not to be taken advantage of by a boss who expects you to do work at home, put in extra time, etc., with no compensation. She's right, as usual. You should do these things of your own accord because you want to and not because they are demanded by an unscrupulous employer. And she's right in saying these things are harder to do if you have young children at home and other obligations. But the principle remains. Doing extra, even a little extra, which is easy, makes a big difference in success. Always do your best to exceed expectations.

Cooperate and don't budge

At first these may sound contradictory, but they are not. Cooperation and service are two of the easiest ways to succeed. I wonder why people find them to be so hard? My guess is that most people are so absorbed in themselves that they don't take the split second it requires to think about what the customer (teacher, parent, friend, child) might be thinking or feeling and how he or she would like you to act. It is so *easy* to put yourself in their place, to remember how you were treated at a restaurant, or on the phone with some agency, or in a bank, or a checkout line at a store. People respond to such thoughtfulness by returning to your business, by tipping, by complimenting you to your boss. It takes very little effort to ask someone if they need help with something, with directions in a hallway or at an elevator, with a wheelchair or groceries or with a child. And the result is that people feel cared about, tended to, looked after – just like you'd like to feel in the same situation. Did you know it takes fewer muscles to smile than it does to frown?

But *don't budge* from your basic beliefs – about yourself, about honesty, fairness, doing the right thing. Stick up for what you believe and quit the job if it makes you compromise your values or feel bad about yourself, or put out a less-than-high quality product or service. Success often means having the courage of your convictions to walk away from unethical, illegal, slimy, or untenable situations.

Buy what you can afford

Success for me also means not worrying about paying bills, not overstretching my budget. It means totally paying off credit cards each month rather than carrying a balance (at high interest rates). It means owing nobody money if I can possibly help it. Of course when you first start out you will buy things on time, pay off a car over years, maybe get a student loan and eventually a mortgage that may take a long time to finish paying.

But if you save a certain portion of your money, you will sleep better at night with the knowledge that you are not indebted financially to anyone. You can even get ahead enough to mess around in the stock market like we do, or pay for your own kids' college education, or have money ready for an unforeseen emergency.

Vote for yourself

I can think of at least five significant occasions where I succeeded by voting for myself: in elementary school when I wanted to be a crossing guard, in high school for a particular award, in college for passing my comprehensive oral exams in religion, and later in my career when I got accredited in two major organizations. These were not just games. I really thought I should get the things and had worked darned hard to qualify for them. The point is that if *you* don't think you are qualified, deserving, prepared, trained, ready – then no one else may either.

The formula

As I thought about this issue of success being easier than most people think, the following formula occurred to me:

Work. Most people dislike their jobs. I have always *loved* mine. Find work you really like. Then *do* it. Do it well, and do more than is expected so you will be expert at it. Grandpa has said my entire life, much to my annoyance, "If you want to eat, you got to work." And it's true, even if you win the lottery. So you might as well spend that one-third of your life on the job enjoying what you have to do to make enough money to live the way you want.

Tenacity. Through thick and thin, stressed-out times and fun, dealing with teachers/bosses who may be distant and aloof, and with teachers/bosses who are supportive – stick with your dream. See *beyond* any adversities. Hang in there for the long run. Don't let adversities run you off. Outlast them. You already know that persistence pays off in success.

Commitment. This is different from tenacity. This means promising yourself you will follow through to get what you want by going the extra ten feet, showing up early, raising your hand when volunteers are needed, keeping your name visible. It means putting your integrity and honesty above even losing your job. It means doing the right thing, no matter what. (And Mom and I will be there for you if the going gets tough for doing just that.)

Practice. Like Babe Ruth – keep on swinging. Like the ice skaters you watch – get up when you fall. But don't swing randomly. Learn from the falls. Take notes. Get somebody to critique you, give you feedback (coaching) on how to improve what you're doing. If you're not constantly improving what you do, you're falling behind.

Risk. Take chances doing something a new way, make a humble suggestion, express an opinion, try something different. Again, these are easy things that lead to success. That's how most great inventors found new things – they purposefully or accidentally combined ingredients in odd, strange, weird, unheard-of ways. Like Ruth, you'll strike out a lot on your way to setting records. Like Spielberg, people may think you're a nerd or a little goofy on your way to the bank. You did this with soccer and actually served as a model for me to risk looking at a new job.

Luck. Sometimes success depends on being in the right place at the right time with the right person. It is important to be open to the gifts life

gives us and to make the most of them, grate-
fully sharing them with others less lucky.

Forgiveness. This may be the most important el-
ement in success. It is important to forgive others and to forgive yourself. Hateful, resentful
people seldom succeed. People who are forgiving live longer and better with less stress and
fewer problems. Nobody's perfect. And our family is a perfect example. We forgive each other
at least once a day for something or other. At
least you've had a lot of practice at it, along with
the next one.

Humor. A trait that goes along with forgiveness,
humor is a requirement of those who succeed. It
is the ability to see your achievement in the long
term and not to take yourself or your successes
and failures with "terminal seriosity." Again, our
family provides lots of experience in this area.

These last two traits will be important when,
in the course of your success, someone dislikes
you or what you are doing.

Celebrate. Remember to celebrate your successes, no matter how small or large. Every time I take another step toward getting a book off to the publisher, or an article out, or another revision of the series script, I celebrate in some way. Run. See a movie. Go out to dinner. Call a friend. Relax and do nothing. Go on a great vacation.

I hope you can see that success is relatively easy, given the competition out there that is usually unwilling to do the above things. Now this does not mean that if you stand still and do nothing you will become a zillionaire, or that if you merely do the expected you will be rewarded with fame and fortune. Success requires persistence, commitment, unswerving devotion to the goal, years of education, and a willingness to accept critique and direction from others. It means the discipline of study, saving your money, and being prudent in how you spend your time and resources. It requires a willingness to put in long hours and do extra things. But it also means really enjoying what you do in your life, having a sense of humor about both failure *and* success.

You will have some of both, Meem, but ultimately you will be successful in whatever you choose to do. How do I know that? You have incredibly good interpersonal skills. You listen exceptionally well and hear the feelings below the words. You know how to be pleasant, and you know how to stick up for what you believe in without budging. You have tenacity and commitment as shown in your school work, sports, and friendships.

Actually, you are successful already. You have great friends. You are excellent academically. You are a volleyball star, an upcoming soccer athlete, a good writer and thinker. Most importantly, you are a loving, generous person who cares a lot about people and ideas. You will make a difference in the lives of many people, and you will leave the world a better place than it was when you arrived here, maybe even in a significant way. For me, that is the most important definition of success.

Watch out world. Here comes the Meemer.

five

MOTHER

You and Mom just had your 400th altercation of the weekend. These all started about four years ago when your very first hormone woke up from 12 years of dormancy and bounced through your body like a steel ball through a pinball machine, dinging off your brain, your pituitary, your ovaries, and your feet, disappearing down into your psyche, where it continues to ring up loud point totals from time to emotional time.

It has been both interesting and distressing for me to watch. Interesting, because no matter what strategy I suggest for avoidance or mediation, the conflict flares at what must be genetic levels. Distressing, because I know how much you love each other underneath it all and how puzzling this must be for you. This last time, though, in a rare glimpse of budding insight, you gave me a bewildered look and asked, "Why do we *do* this, Dad?"

Here's my theory. There exists an undiscovered DNA molecule that is passed from mother to daughter which serves to bond them primally for the first 11 or 12 years of their existence together. The appearance of the first adolescent hormone, however, triggers this DNA molecule in the daughter to do everything it can to *break* that carefully cemented bond, sometimes gently, sometimes noisily. At the same time, the mother's DNA molecule is triggered by the daughter's behavior and sets out to do the same thing. So adolescent years with mothers and daughters are often spent pinging between closeness and distance, anger and intimacy. This is evolutionarily necessary or mothers and daughters would *never* separate but continue like the mama monkey with the baby monkey on her back until the mama was in an electric wheelchair pulling the daughter along on her wheeled walker and the world would die out because nobody would propagate. Ever.

In addition to that normal genetic activity working to separate you, you have what you may believe is the additional burden of living with a mother with cancer. Now the truth is that *every* daughter has a mother with *something*, cancer or otherwise, that the kid has to work through. Actually, if you had to pick, cancer is better than say, alcoholism, or schizophrenia, or abuse, or just plain meanness. That aside, I *do* think it is important to look at your particular circumstance from the point of view of a totally objective, fully rational, peripherally involved party (that would be me). So here goes.

You said recently that you can't remember a time when Mom wasn't sick, and I believe you. She discovered she had leukemia just as you were becoming sentient, about age five. She immediately got the bone marrow transplant in Seattle and worked part-time after that till we met and got married, when she was in complete remission. Not long after that she relapsed and we've been dealing with drugs, chemotherapy, and side effects since then.

It is important for me to tell you that I remember a time when Mom wasn't sick, a time when she was actively working as a school psychologist, jogging three times a week, taking vitamins as her only medication, and cooking breakfast and dinner for us every morning and night. That's the woman I fell in love with and married. It's still the woman I kiss good night every night. In fact, to be fair, Mom isn't all that different now, except in stamina. Her erratic platelet counts, unpredictable pain, and exhausting fatigue preclude her working and jogging, but if she conserves her energy she manages to get you to school and back, get us fed, and still maintain her sense of humor about her illness and us. But my guess is that it's the previous, nonfatigued mother you get glimpses of every now and then; the mother that a part of you remembers and yearns to have back.

Because somewhere buried in the memory bank of your psyche are indelibly encoded pictures of a young, pretty, loving woman who doted entirely on you and the cat (in that order). She raised you single-handedly after your father left. She allowed the old couple who lived next door to you in Indiana (Mamaw and Papaw) to shower you with their love and attention as well. She was a strong, independent woman from a strong, independent Texas family who taught you in those early formative years to be the caring, loving, giving, and forgiving person you are now. The "strong" and "independent" seems to have rubbed off on you as well.

Though you have no memory of it, I need to tell you that Mom was a very competent professional woman, a leader in her field, who started and supervised an entire psychology department in a rural school system. When I met her she was highly respected in her peer group of school psychologists, even though she was working half-time and recovering from the incredibly debilitating effects of the bone marrow transplant.

Her early imprinting on you is evident in your best characteristics – your ability to think clearly; discern emotional matters; and empathize with people and help mediate solutions, understanding issues beyond your years. Your love of children and animals is identical to hers, and you are good with both because you are trustworthy and trusting – as is Mom.

You are also, like her, a survivor. You have amazing persistence and the same characteristic ability to keep going against all odds. For Mom this was exemplified in a life-and-death struggle with the leukemia and the bone marrow transplant. I have seen you act similarly every time you try out for something and don't get it or submit something and get turned down. You bounce back and try another approach to the same thing, or you go after something else.

Two other things have happened to add fuel to the genetic conflict between you both. The first is that Mom's sister and I came into the picture just as Mom was doing worse, being sicker and weaker. I took up a lot of the slack in those early years as Mom got through the various treatments, the side effects of which made her weak, forgetful, and tired all the time. Aunt Kay moved her own highly successful business here and posed a role model of wealth and competence. Contrasted with Kay and me, with our extremely complex jobs and successful careers, you may have seen Mom as less competent or valuable. Let me assure you that Kay and I (and you too, actually) have it easy compared to Mom. None of us has to juggle the complexities of managing a household (including an active adolescent and a demanding Abyssinian), keeping us fed and in clean clothes, while at the same time coordinating medications, physician appointments and orders, weekly blood tests, and the constant worry that the pain in our knee or back or head means the cancer is advancing and death is one click nearer. But what appears to you as her inability to keep up with you annoys you and feeds the genetic chemicals to provide more grounds for separation.

The second thing is that the chemicals on that adolescence gene serve both as an anesthetic and an amnesiac: the anesthetic numbs you to your feelings about all of the above and the amnesiac makes you forget everything that happened before about age 13. The chemicals pave the way for narcissism, the constant examination of yourself and your body and your behavior, as though you were the known center of the universe and no one else, particularly parents, mattered. Especially Mother.

Be assured this is perfectly normal. Whether the mom has cancer or diabetes, or was divorced and is remarrying, or hasn't worked but is going to work, or works full-time and is never home – all of this has to happen. You have to intensely focus on yourself to find out something about who you are (separate from us) so you can survive later when you are *really* separate from us, whether at college, or working, or married, or you've outlived us. The tightly intertwined vines have to be pulled away from each other to follow their own directions, sometimes broken or painfully cut, so that both of you can go on with the rest of your lives, maybe intertwining in different ways later, when you've both grown some more.

So for now those genetic chemicals will probably allow you to see Mom only as tired and hurting, with a less-than-optimal memory due to the chemo, radiation, and meds she's been through. They may not let you see or believe the incredible strength and courage she exhibits daily in forcing her stiff, pained body to get up, stand in the hot shower until her joints can move, make her hands and arms manipulate makeup and clothes, manage the house and food and our schedules, and spend time "digging in the dirt" to make our yard into a beautifully landscaped garden. In this way, the chemicals protect and anesthetize you from the reality of Mom, which would be too overwhelming for you right now, given the task of separation. If you really got in touch with her struggle you both would want to bond even closer than you were, and, sad to say, that must not happen if you are to approach greater independence.

Part of my frustration is that I hate it when you two fight (or when you and I fight, for that matter). I like you both and it worries me that your last memories of each other might be angry and unaccepting. Like the Garth Brooks song says, "If tomorrow never comes, will she know how much I loved her?" So I've wondered what would happen if you figured out how to "bless" each other. What would that look like? What behavior would it take? Is it possible or desirable?

Blessing in the Bible meant several things. It meant affirming the other person without wanting her to change. It meant accepting the other person as he was in a way that enabled both parties to grow and not be stuck with images of each other from the past. Specifically, Mom's blessing you means her accepting that the two of you are different people and becoming more different as the years go by. You and Mom would realize that your DNA is going to conflict from time to time and, when that happens, you both would remember to disengage and let the chemicals calm down. Blessing Mom would mean your affirming her as she is right now (rather than as you want her to be) and assisting her when you can. Mom's blessing you would mean trusting that those competent, nurturing, loving images of her buried in your memory are in fact the basis of your relationship and that, when the chemicals in both of you have done their job, those memories will resurface to bring you closer in a different kind of relationship. Blessing Mom would mean thanking her for being the kind of person who modeled the traits and behaviors that are now such a part of you, knowing that you will use them in your own way with your own style of being and character.

But maybe this is not possible until the genes in you both have run their course, dinged off each other, accomplished your separation and independence, launched you both into the next phases of your lives, and dissipated out of your systems, allowing you to see each other clearly again.

The fear, of course, is that Mom may die before that happens, but you cannot and must not let that threat deter you from your (and your hormone's) intended course. Interestingly enough, the threat of her death may force those chemicals to do their work more quickly and dissipate sooner, giving you both more time together without the effects of the anesthetic or amnesia.

Who knows? Mom has outlasted all the dire predictions of her healthcare providers for 11 years now, and outlived many of our friends who thought she'd die before they did. At this rate, she'll be around to dote on your own children (at age 26?) and their cat.

It would be interesting to see what would happen if, next time your DNAs collide, you could be grateful and bless the conflict. But, hell, that's probably too Zen for us all. When you and I have arguments, the only thing I'm grateful for is that I know beyond a shadow of a doubt your kids will do this to you when their DNA rebels against yours, and I can't wait to be around to see it. That is the nature of things that grow up and grow beyond us.

In the meantime, as you run through your final two years of high school and on to college, and Mom and I deal with our midlives and decide what to do next, I'll bless you both and be grateful for whatever time we have together.

six

FAIR

"Could I get cancer?" you asked, sitting on the chair in our bedroom as you often do when you are in the mood for philosophical ruminating. This question is usually related to the fear that, like your mother, you will unexpectedly and inexplicably be struck with leukemia at an early age.

Your mother and I both nodded.

"What about colon cancer? Isn't that curable?"

We allowed as how it was, but often involved a colostomy.

"Permanently?" you replied to my comment about pooping through your abdomen into a bag.

"Anything's possible," I said.

"But it's not *fair*," you whine in the voice you know I hate, that insipid, helpless, two-year-old, do-something-to-fix-it-because-I-can't-do-any-thing-about-it-myself voice.

"That's true," I agreed, smiling at the knowledge that you were finally getting it, understanding at a gut level the concept that we are all in this together because we are all exiting the same way.

"But it's not fair! Whatever you do, something's going to get you."

"Right," I replied. "The question isn't, 'Am I going to die?' That's a stupid question! We're *all* going to die. The question is, 'What are you going to do in the meantime?' And the best you can do is to stack the cards in your direction every chance you get. You can eat right, exercise, and take care of your body. You know this is my code for stay the hell away from drugs, alcohol, and that bane of my existence – teenage boys whose goal in life is to give you a sexually transmitted disease that will make you sterile or dead.

Your mother pipes up from her side of the bed. "Even then," she says, "you could still get hit by a truck." This you know to be her code for what will happen if you ever get behind the wheel of a car – which you are planning to do in two months when you turn 15.

So we talk about diseases, how you get them and how you don't, on the educational theory that repetition over time equals knowledge and, hopefully, terror, and end the discussion with something about volleyball and how we will get you to practice that night. It is a typical Michal-discussion, the kind I love, where we joust around major life-threatening issues and dodge and weave through mundane activities like who to vote for, what your grandmother died of, and whether you should go in early tomorrow for help with math.

But there is more to the conversation in my head, of course, and that's why I'm writing these letters to you, so here it is.

Life *is* unfair. There's nothing fair about it. As you know well from living in our family, bad things happen to good people. Mom did nothing to *deserve* the leukemia. Our friend Bernadette did nothing to deserve the breast cancer that killed her. Maxwell our clergy-cat did nothing to deserve getting old and losing control of his body functions and having to be put to sleep. As you have learned in your long 14 years, we get a lot of undeserved suffering in our lives, and ultimately that suffering will end in our death.

But the opposite is also true. We get a tremendous amount of undeserved joy as well. We didn't *deserve* to end up as a family together. The three of us could have ended up living separate lives, never knowing each other, never loving each other, never being there to support each other through the successes and failures of our family life together. Or we could have ended up with different people in very different circumstances. Likewise, you didn't *deserve* to get a healthy, athletic body with good teeth and hair and a face like an angel. You didn't deserve a winning ticket in the genetic lottery, but you got it anyway, and sometimes people less fortunate than you may think that is unfair.

So it's true life is not fair – but it's equally unfair in both directions, in the direction of joy and the direction of sorrow.

So what does that mean for you personally, or, as you would say – "And your point would be?"

My point would be back to what I said when

you were sitting on the chair in our bedroom, that we *can* stack the deck in our direction to the best of our ability. Just because life isn't fair doesn't mean *I* can't be fair. Put another way, the unfairness of life does not give me license or permission or justification to be unfair.

Now I realize that this idea goes against every TV show you watch, from MTV to the hot evening soaps, where the assumption is that people should get even with people who do them wrong, return hatred for hatred, injustice for injustice, "an eye for an eye." But the "eye for an eye" bit was, in fact, a plea for fairness, not a statement in support of revenge. In an age when you could literally slaughter another person for putting out your eye, this law *restricted* the response to *only* putting out the other person's eye. Jesus, of course, is quoted as saying to "turn the other cheek" and we'll talk about that at length later. The Apostle Paul, always the pragmatist, said to be nice to people who hate you because it will drive them nuts. More precisely, he said, "because by doing so you will pour burning coals on their heads." Frankly, I like that. And it works.

The truth is, rather than being fair or unfair, life is neutral.

"The rain falls on the just and the unjust." Don't take it personally.

"Bad things happen to good people and good things happen to bad people." And vice versa.

"*Caca pasa.*" Texas State Motto.

"Practice random acts of kindness." Kindness is random anyway.

In fact, the neutrality of life allows me to exercise choice in a way that would be impossible otherwise. Suppose, for a minute, that life was always fair and that you and I always got exactly what we deserved. When we thought bad thoughts or did bad things in the heat of argument or accident, we would be immediately punished by life. When we did good things we would be immediately rewarded. You would receive only the amount of money you earned through fair work around the house or babysitting or a job, and you would be required to pay your share of household expenses along with performing an equal share of the chores.

Great, huh?

I don't think so.

When I worked at the penitentiary, I used to hear inmates complain about the unfairness of their sentences, nearly all of which were plea-bargained – time reduced for pleading guilty and saving the State the cost of a trial. My comment was that "Life is unfair and it's a darned good thing. How much time would you be doing if you got what you really deserved?"

You see, the problem with fairness as we lament it is that it allows no room for forgiveness or mercy or understanding or compassion or unconditional giving or love. Because all those things are inherently *unfair*. There's nothing fair about forgiving each other for hurts or name calling or deceit or wrongdoing against the other. There's nothing fair about parents getting little things for their kids or saving for their education or protecting them from the real or imagined realities (and horrors) of life they will soon enough have to shoulder themselves.

Because, ultimately, love is not fair. That's why we love each other even when we don't deserve it, maybe *especially* when we don't deserve it. Love transcends fairness and unfairness, embraces and engulfs them both, transforms them and us into something better than what we deserve. It allows us to be just – even when attacked by unjust people – to tell the truth in the face of lies, to return mercy for judgmentalness, kindness for hatred, silence for loud condemnation.

You're absolutely right when you say that life is unfair, sweetie pie. Just remember that it's equally unfair in both directions, thank God, and that love is even more unfair than life.

seven

DOING IT

It seems that the boyfriend of one of your best friends "did it." Apparently Lynn broke up with James (not their real names) because Lynn wouldn't do it – go all the way, have sexual intercourse with him. Then after they broke up, James started dating another girl at school for a short time and they did it and he broke up with her and now is back dating Lynn. This raises some interesting questions for me and, hopefully, for you.

Why did Lynn go back with James after he dumped her for someone who would let him use her for sex then be dumped like yesterday's garbage so he could return to good old Lynn? Does he think Lynn's values are better than the other girl's? Does he think he's now somehow superior or more experienced (therefore more mature) than Lynn because he's done it and she hasn't? Will he begin to pressure Lynn to do it? Is this a matter of conquests for James? Names he can drop to other guys? Referrals for a good time? What will happen to Lynn's reputation now that she's back with James and subject to rumors that she's doing it with him?

In any case, Meem, the circles are getting closer. You start out knowing someone whose boyfriend did it with someone else. Next you will know a close girlfriend who has done it with her boyfriend. Finally some boy will be wanting you to do it with him. And finally, finally, you will want to do it with some boy.

What to do about all this? I wish I knew. But since I don't know, I can only talk about the issues and trust that you will come to the best decision for yourself. You always do. As I have observed about you in other areas, you have the incredible knack of knowing the right thing to do and accomplishing it.

One issue is how you know you are ready to have sex with someone. There are several ways to evaluate this.

Set an arbitrary age

"I won't have sex till I'm 36," is where your parents think is a good place to start. For right now you might want to say, "I will have sex when I get to college." That has the presumed value of waiting till you are out of adolescence and have begun to acquire enough experience of the world and yourself to handle the emotional component of sex, and enough intelligence (not to mention motor skills) to accurately use birth control devices. The upside of setting an arbitrary age is that it gives you an excuse or an explanation based on your own decision, and if a guy wants to discount your decision and ignore your values then you know he thinks more of himself and his own wants than he does of you and yours.

Blame your parents

"My parents will kill me if I do it." Of course this is true. Bazooka Dad will off any boy who touches you inappropriately. So if you don't want to take the weight for the decision right now, it's fine with me. You'll have plenty of time to take responsibility for this decision later in life. Blame us for imposing unrealistic, stupid, out-of-date, hypocritical, unfair, rigid rules on your personal behavior. This method helps get you off the hook and allows you to buy time to make your own decision and go with one of the other strategies.

Wait to decide until it's absolutely necessary
This means: "I'll know the right time to have sex with the right guy." It avoids committing to any course of behavior except the spur of the moment. It is like saying, "I'll learn how to swim when the boat capsizes." Or, "I'll put the helmet on before the bike hits the ground." Or the condom. This method puts off thinking about what to do until you are in the midst of the crisis of passion or the pressure of feelings. It critically reduces the amount of time you have to make a reasoned decision to something like three nano-seconds.

AAAANNNNNHHHKKKK. Thank you for playing.

It is nearly impossible to make rational decisions in the heat of passion. That's what passion is *for* – to avoid making rational decisions and get on with reproducing the species. My only advice here is that I seldom make good decisions under that kind of pressure. I usually like to sleep *on* such decisions, rather than *with* them.

Decide to wait until you're married

I know. I know. I know. Everyone will say this is the stupidest, dumbest, most unrealistic of all. Kids who do this are ridiculed as conservative, chicken, immature, babies, or possibly gay. People say you ought to have the experience, you'll never find a *guy* who's a virgin, and what does it really matter anyway?

The truth is I could give you ten good reasons to wait until you're married – and ten good reasons not to. I'm sure you're smart enough to do the same and they'd likely be similar reasons in each category. The only point in deciding this is that it presumably postpones sex until after college, and there are pluses and minuses to that as well.

So what to do? As you might guess, rather than having an answer or answers, all I can do to help here is provide a framework in which to think about the issue and trust that you will figure out the right thing to do for you.

One of things I thought about was, "Why is this such a big deal?" And, although in the larger scheme of things it really isn't, there are some reasons that sexuality and intercourse are endowed with such major importance.

The double standard

Due to some genetic remnant of Neanderthal brain cells left over from the days when women were chattel (property), there still exists what is called the double standard. This means that boys can have sex with as many girls as they can convince it's okay to do it with – but girls have to be virgins when they marry. You might wonder how there are any left?

You already know that this totally violates my rabid demand for sexual equality. Why should girls be held to different standards than boys? (Aside from the fact that girls are generally smarter, more mature, and have no need to prove

their macho worth through sexual conquests –
but who's prejudiced?)

The subtle implication of the double standard
is that you may be judged as "promiscuous" for
having sexual partners while boys will be con-
sidered "experienced." Slut versus Stud. It is
totally unfair, but it does not mean that girls
should demand equality by having as many conquests as boys just for the sake of numbers. It
does mean that your reputation will be evaluated
by a different standard than the boys', in this
culture. And your reputation is something you
have to live with in the lonely hours of the night,
as well as when you wake up and face yourself in
the mirror each morning. And that is a big deal,
not because of the macho boys or the cultural
standard, but because it effects your own self-
esteem – out of which most other decisions are
made.

It is irretrievable

Once you've done it you can't go back to the place
where you've never done it. You can't erase the
tape and start over, or put it in reverse and make
it not have happened, or replay it with a differ-

ent outcome. Once you go there, you've been there. In accordance with the double standard, adolescent girls almost universally report that they regret having given in to the now-vanished boyfriend – wish they could go back to the time when they hadn't had sex – while adolescent boys are pleased with the conquest and ready to go on to the next one.

But one might reasonably say, "So what?" You have to have sex for the first time sometime, so why not get it over with, have the experience, add it to your list of things you've done (like skiing and New York), and get on with your life?

The answer is, again, it is irretrievable, and those of us who have crossed that boundary (i.e., your parents) would like you to be older than 19 when you do. Why? Partly because of the next issue.

Bodies and emotions are not equal

The problem for adolescents is that their bodies are evolutionarily ready to reproduce the species – but their emotions have to live in the age of cyberspace. The prime childbearing years are between about 16 and 32, when bodies are young, tough, and agile enough to keep up with toddlers. So your gene pool is shouting for you to have sex to preserve the race from extinction. It is as though a little prehistoric gene in your brain keeps a radar lookout for opportunities (i.e., babes, hunks, stud muffins) hoping ultimately for a coupling with the best and the brightest to make Darwin happy. But society has changed from Darwin's jungle to one where you have to have a graduate school education and a career to be able to afford just living single. So your rational side has to keep yelling at the gene to shut up and let you put off babies for another ten or so years while you get all your education without the obstruction (or derailment) of children. Furthermore, your emotions and feelings aren't nearly as ready for sex as your genes are. Remember your genes have been around for thousands of years with lots of encoded experience with this, while your emotions have only been here for 16 years and are relatively new and overwhelmed.

STDs, cancer, and death
You already know about STDs from school, but I do need to reinforce to you the information from

physician friends of mine who see large numbers of young women unable to bear children because of fairly common STDs such as chlamydia, which can scar fallopian tubes and render them ineffective, or which can infect ovaries which may have to be removed, making the person sterile. AIDS is the big scare right now, worse than pregnancy and STDs, because, although it is becoming a long-term chronic illness, it still ultimately destroys your immune system and causes death. But the bigger worry might be cancer of the cervix, since there seems to be a correlation between early intercourse and a high incidence of that disease.

There really is no such thing as safe sex, emotionally or physically. And the truth is nobody is ever "ready" to have sex the first time, but you can be more ready or less ready, more informed about how to take precautions and practice them to prevent pregnancy and disease, or uninformed and unready to take such precautions. My only wish is that you be more than less ready. More prepared than less prepared, so that it doesn't "just happen."

Sex doesn't "just happen." I believe that that is a giant cop-out, an excuse, a refusal to take responsibility for setting it up and doing it. Each of us is smart enough to know what situations we're getting into and the likelihood that the deck is stacked in favor of having sex or not. Just remember that, even at the last minute, you can say "No" and have that honored. (The parachute again.) I just want it to be on your terms, when you're as ready as possible, with no coercion (emotional or physical).

Oh yeah, and pregnancy

Adolescents get pregnant mainly because they think they can't. Old teen tales still abound about what works and what doesn't work, what prevents conception and what does not. Although you are exceptionally well informed on these issues, if you have any doubts ask someone. Parents believe that teenage girls get pregnant if they get downwind from an adolescent boy. This is not true, of course. You have to be upwind where the sperm are expert swimmers.

We worry about stuff we didn't have to contend with when we were your age. Although date rape happened, people didn't have easily available drugs that knock out the girl so she has no recall of being raped. It's a strange world where we have to remind you to get your own drink, open your own can, and be certain you really know and trust your date – and the people at the party – to lessen the chance that this occurs.

So – what to do? Here are some suggestions, most of which you've thought about already, but it never hurts to reinforce them.

Trust yourself

You've already had one situation where you needed to have a talk with the boy about the depth of each other's feelings. I really admire your ability, first, to identify the issues and feelings inside yourself, and second, to have the courage and assertiveness to do something about it immediately. You seem to trust your intuition on things, or at least you seem to know what your intuition is saying and to check it out with a reality test before leaping into something from which it might be difficult to extricate yourself.

Behavior over time

This is the best predictor of commitment and responsibility in a relationship. If the person is

trustworthy, caring, treats you as an equal, returns your affection, and is, above all, a friend,
you might begin to imagine how sex will be a part
of the larger context of your relationship. How
much time? I don't know. I do know that dating
in high school was the normal place to experi-
ment with falling in love – whatever that meant
or still means – but that I did it so often that I
seldom went with anyone long enough to get a
real picture of behavior over time. That didn't
really happen till after college.

Sex changes the relationship

Whether you are 24 or 42, having sex is indelible. No matter what people may tell you about
it being the same as kissing or shaking hands,
the vulnerable emotional component and physical bonding raise expectations that both will
stay around (to raise the kids, if that little gene
has its way). In the context of a long-term relationship, sex becomes a way of affirming that
commitment to staying around as a couple
(even if you fool the gene by using birth control
devices).

Talk about it

At the pen, inmates used to say, "Do the time. Don't let the time do you." I would paraphrase that to say, "Have the sex. Don't let the sex have you." Talk about it with your potential partner when you think you're ready. Talk with other people to bounce off whether or not you are ready. You wouldn't choose a college, buy a car, or take a trip to Europe without planning for it. Why is sex different?

Finally, the four strategies at the beginning of this piece are only to buy time. Eventually you will find the right person at the right time and, hopefully, sex will be enjoyable, fun, satisfying – and not nearly the big deal everybody said it was.

In the meantime, I trust your judgment and, in spite of my prejudices, I am willing to be relatively objective if you want to bounce stuff off me. Mom too. Besides, Rhonda the Psychic said you wouldn't do it till your senior year in college when you found someone you loved and who loved you.

Whatever.

I just love you and want you to be safe, though I know that is a fantasy that diminishes with every passing day of your growing life. In sexuality, as in every other area, you are moving out of our span of control and into your own. I trust that you'll handle this as you handle every other dilemma – with the care, concern, and self-integrity that characterize your choices.

Even in the midst of screaming genes.

eight

MONEY

You were not thrilled about setting up your first checking account. As we filled out the forms, you gave me that "This is a dad thing" look for wanting you to do this. You could not imagine needing such a thing and you were rightly worried about keeping track of the checks and having money to put in the account in the first place. But by the time we got home you had figured out that you could split the birthday and Christmas money you usually put in savings and put half of it in checking. You have done a great job of building up your savings account, by the way, dumping in babysitting

money and checks from relatives and never
wanting to take money out.

You and I have had a few major blow-ups over
the years and I would bet they have all been related to money. You wanted something (clothes,
a game, or a toy) and I thought it was outrageously priced, a ridiculous fad, or a brand name
that was being used to extort money from parents being blackmailed by their kids. When I was
a kid (don't you love that phrase?) it was Gant
shirts and white Levi's and Weejuns. Now it's
Doc Marten's and Victoria's Secret and GAP. Or
at least it was. Now it is a *car*.

Nobody told me about the passage of that
Federal legislation that says every kid is automatically entitled to a car at age 16. What a surprise. I was still operating off the assumption that
cars arrived when you *needed* them and *you paid
for them* – like I did when I graduated from college and was getting married. Of course, that was
in the days when the major driving hazards were
pterodactyls and volcanic ash. As usual, after
much discussion, we both reverted to the relatively reasonable people we are and mediated a
compromise. If it seems that you need a car in

the next year or so, depending on your driving ability and how school is going, maybe you'll get Mom's car and she'll get another one. We'll see. In the meantime, both the checking account and the car provide the opportunity to talk about money (since you will be paying half of your car insurance).

It is important to know where you stand with money before you have to deal with it, either by not having enough, or by having so much you don't know what to do with it, though you probably don't think the latter is a problem.

I grew up with Depression-era parents who operate off the notion that there is *never* enough money in your savings account and that you always have to worry about saving for "a rainy day" – or in their case decade (1929-39). But I also grew up in the financially abundant '60s, worked hard to build a career, and now live in the equally bountiful '90s. As a result, I carry with me not only the constant worry about not having enough, which makes me save and plan for that rainy day (wisdom teeth, furnace croaking, deck rotting out, emergency trips to aging parents), but also the experience of making enough to live well and enjoy it (first-class vacations, organic groceries, cool car). Hopefully, I will pass along both of those prejudices to you and you will have to figure out how best to balance them for yourself.

At 16, money looks like the answer to everything. Hell, at 49 it looks like the answer to everything. We both fantasize about winning the lottery, writing a *New York Times* bestseller, or getting a movie contract. Indeed, any of those would take some of the pressure off the immediate future – college and retirement. And while money sometimes helps address a problem, it is always a temporary answer, never a permanent one.

Though adolescent magazines and TV shows and peer culture may tell you that the purpose of money is money and more money, that the accumulation of wealth is *the* goal, I would argue that, in fact, money is not an end in itself. It is a *means* to an end. This is a biggie. Most people don't get it the first time around. I'll say it again. Money is not the end goal of the journey, though it might help you reach that goal. What you have to decide is where you want to go, and, perhaps more importantly, what kind of person you want to be while you're getting there. After those two decisions, the issue of money is a distant third.

There are lots of theories about money.

Ben Franklin

Ben Franklin said, "Neither a borrower nor a lender be." This means doing your best to be financially independent. I have followed this rule, paid cash for nearly everything, and limited debt to the mortgage on the house. I figure if I don't have the cash for it, I don't need it; and if I do need it or really want it, then it will be worth waiting and saving for. This means paying off credit cards every month rather than running a balance that collects interest at high rates (and not charging things on my credit card that I can't pay off each month). Likewise, I have never loaned anyone money without a written legal agreement to repay me. This has kept me out of trouble with friends from time to time. A close college friend called once to ask to borrow a thousand dollars. I told him I'd consider it when I received the legal papers designating the date of payback and what happened if he didn't pay it back. I never got the papers and never heard from him again. Ever. Some close friend.

Ben Franklin and I believe that it is important to be realistic when dealing with money, which means planning to spend only what I know we've got and if we get more – great. In other words, *plan for the worst and hope for the best.* Assume you've only got the money you can see in front of you (or in your checking account) and be happily surprised if an extra check arrives.

Worth

Another theory about money is that it is a measure of your value. People ask, "What's she *worth?*" as though her bank account determined her stature in the community, or the condition of her soul. Bill Gates of Microsoft was "worth" many billions of dollars last year. But I would argue that his real stature is reflected in the huge amounts he's giving away to libraries across the country to get them computer efficient, and in the many other charities he and his workers support. The truth is that what you're *worth* has nothing to do with what you *have*. You can have a lot of money and be lacking in compassion. To be fair, you can *not* have a lot of money and be lacking in compassion as well. As that children's album we used to play says, "It's not how much you're born with, it's what you do with what you've got." You can be middle class and generous; you can be rich and worthless.

The Bible

Though you'd never know it from listening to sermons around pledge time, the biblical theory of money has nothing to do with guilt. It has to do with *stewardship*. The idea is that God made the earth and said to us, "Here. It's the best thing I've done. You take care of it for me, as my caretaker (steward). Make sure you water the plants and feed the cat and clean up the dog dumps and pull the weeds and, while you're at it, if you can make it prettier, give it a shot. Here are the keys to the world. I'll be back."

Then God leaves for a long and well-deserved vacation – with us in charge. As God's stewards. Now a steward doesn't *own* the thing she's stewarding any more than you own the kids you babysit. We're sort of babysitting the earth for God till whenever.

We're also babysitting God's money. Just like every other resource in the world, money is put into our hands to do with as we will as God's stewards. In the New Testament parable of the talents (Matthew 25:14–30), a master goes away and leaves his servants with different amounts of money till he gets back. Now after a long time the master of those servants came back and settled accounts with them. How good a steward has each one been? Turns out the first guy put his in the bank and returned the original amount with interest. "Not bad," the king says and welcomes him into the Kingdom. Second guy put his into computer stocks and tripled the original amount. "Good job," says the king and welcomes him into the Kingdom. Third guy just buried his in the ground so nobody would steal it. He dusts off the coffee can and hands back the original amount, proud of himself for not wasting it or losing it. *"Dummkopf!"* the king yells, lapsing into German for "stupidhead." "You're outta here," the king points downward and condemns him to Hell, "where men weep and gnash their teeth."

And – as you have taught me to say – your point would be? The point in this theory of money is that a good steward takes the "money" (or the land, or the body you've been given, or the intellect, or the skill, or the actual wealth) and puts it to use. She doesn't bury it in the ground for fear of losing it. She risks it in the marketplace of school and friends and family and ideas and conflict and sacrifice (giving it away) in order to return it to its rightful owner even more worthy then when it was first given to her to watch over as a steward.

This theory is reflected in church when they take the offerings up to the altar and we stand and say, "Hey! You forgot my change!" No, that's after church when we go to Starbuck's. In church we say, "All things come of Thee, O Lord. And of *thine own* have we given Thee." Or, in like modern like English: "Like it's all yours anyway and we're like giving some of it back. Like."

There's one more interesting postscript from that master story, and it's a zinger. At the end, after the two who gave back more are drinking smoothies in the Kingdom, and the guy who buried the coffee can is gnashing in Hell, Jesus says, "For to she who has, even more will be given and she will have in abundance, but from him who has not, even what he has will be taken away." Wow. There's a showstopper. For me that means that the more generous I am with God's money and the more I work responsibly to increase God's bank account as a steward of it – the more it will fill up. If I foolishly blow it, lose it, hoard it, spend it selfishly or to the detriment of others, even what I have will be taken away.

In another story, Jesus added a little extra twist when he said, "Where your money is, there will your heart be also." Funny he didn't say it the other way around: "Where your heart is, there will your money be." That's because, contrary to popular belief, Jesus was a hard-shelled realist. He knew that actions speak louder than words and that people in fact spend their limited resources (time and money) on what is most important to them. In the psychedelic '60s, Jesus dropped a poster on us that said, "Could God tell you were a Christian by looking at your checkbook?" Interesting thought, especially now that you have one. It was right next to the other poster that said, "If you were on trial for being a Christian, would there be enough evidence to convict you?" The '60s were awesome that way, making you 'fess up to your phoniness unless you were really doing something that made a difference.

So the biblical theory of money as something we've been given to watch over as stewards means it isn't really ours anyway, and we're supposed to use it and improve on it so that we give back more than we were given at the start. It sees money as a part of the proof for what we say we believe. If actions speak louder than words, currency speaks loudest of all.

New Age

There is a current New Age theory that says, "Follow your bliss and the money will be there." I like the sound of this one, but it does smack of narcissism (self-centeredness) just a tad. If I followed my bliss and quit work tomorrow to write full time, we'd have to move to a condo, sell one of the cars, never eat out, buy fewer things, you'd be on your own for college, and none of us would have healthcare insurance for little things like your teeth and Mom's medications.

Fortunately, I am lucky to be able to follow part of my bliss at work and get paid for it while

I follow my other bliss at home writing. So far, we've only seen a little money from the home bliss so we'll keep the day job a few more years. But the theory is instructive. Many people take a job just for the money and hate it as they daily waste their lives making lots of bucks. Once again we're back to the stewardship issue. We are just as much stewards of our lives (and bodies and time) as we are of money. Following your bliss means doing the thing that uses the "talents" you've been given, which turns out to be the very thing that is most fulfilling and gratifying. If you do this, in the words of the Rolling Stones, while you might not get what you want, "you just might find, you get what you *need*."

Dad's theory

Based on all of the above, here's my own theory of money. It's a simple threefold concept: Amass. Give. Spend. In that order.

Amass. Andrew Carnegie thought that the first 50 years of a person's life were to be spent amassing all the money you possibly could, so that you could spend the rest of your life giving away as much as possible. I have problems with waiting that long and so have sought to amass and give along the way. Amassing means saving a portion of your paycheck. Every paycheck. This means putting it away like you don't have it and don't want to see it, maybe in a separate account that you can write checks on later. It means being prudent in your purchases, not spending more than you have, being responsible about taking care of monthly payments for college loans, gas and electric, car, and even house payments. Eventually it will mean investing wisely to get the most out of what you've got, not burying it in a coffee can.

You may make mistakes, misjudgments, or things may go wrong temporarily, but the goal is to keep building up and amassing this resource you've been given; you must tend it like you do your body, take good care of it, exercise it to make it stronger, build it up as you work. You must amass it, multiply it like the loaves and the fishes, make it grow in order to be able to do the next thing.

Give. This is the really fun part for me. I love giving money away. I wish I could give away a billion dollars a year – anonymously. Like John Beresford Tipton in the '50s TV show *The Millionaire.* Working on the boards of social agencies like Meals on Wheels or Hospice or People's Community Clinic, I know what a tremendous task lies before them. You've delivered meals with me and you've seen it for yourself. For a whole host of social, political, and economic reasons which we could debate at length, there is an unending stream of people needing everything from food or healthcare to counseling or legal assistance. Social service organizations rely on donations to provide those things.

Jesus said, "The poor you will always have with you." I think he said this not because it is a part of any divine plan to enable people with extra money to have somewhere to donate it, but because he was a realist. He knew that greed would result in poverty – the ultimate in poor stewardship. In fact, you can make the argument that poverty is the measure of how well we're doing as stewards of God's money which has been loaned to us temporarily and entrusted into our bank accounts.

There is a very strange phenomenon that I have noticed over the years, Meem, and I don't quite understand it even yet. I want to tell you about it so you can watch for it yourself. It has happened over and over to me that the more I give/donate, the more money comes my way. Numerous times I've written a check to some agency, and within the week I receive a payment for something, or a gift, or a fee that someone forgot to pay me, or a refund on something that is exactly the amount I gave away. Too weird for words, huh?

Sometimes it's not the exact amount; sometimes it's more, sometimes less. But invariably, the more I give away, the more I make. This is, for me, further evidence that I'm a channel for bucks that aren't *my* bucks. A steward of someone else's stuff. A caretaker. And, strangely enough, one of the ways to make the stuff grow is to give it away.

I think if I were in that parable as the fourth guy, I'd have to tell the king I spent it all. I'd explain that I invested it in Mattel, put my kid through college on Barbie stock, took my wife on a great vacation, visited my ancient parents

and paid for their cable, and gave the rest away
to people and agencies I thought would use it
well. Then I'd hand him an empty coffee can. Be
interesting to see where he'd send me.

Spend. "Life is uncertain. Eat dessert first." This
slogan is my motto for vacation. I love to spend
money on vacating. Gettin' out of Dodge. Going
places and doing things away from home and
work. Balancing out long hours of stressful work
amassing resources with time away not worrying about money at all. I don't like extravagance.
It seems stupid and wasteful to me. Might as well
burn the money as squander it. But I do like convenience and quality and am willing to pay for
both.

In this culture money largely buys you access.
First Class boards first and gets fed full meals on
short flights. You wait for your plane more com-
fortably in the Admiral's Club. Orchestra seats allow you to see and hear better. Cabs are faster than
subways, and sometimes cleaner. The note from
the fancy hotel puts you at the front of the line at
Hard Rock Cafe. Gold means your car is waiting
and heated in the winter, cooled in the summer,

with no stop at the desk. The prep school education may expose you to more things than public
school, and its reputation at least initially gets the
attention of college admissions counselors. If you
have enough money to go to any college you want,
you don't have to compete for admission with those
seeking scholarships. Your transcript starts out in
a different pile. A shorter one.

Money buys access and privilege and it's fun
to play that game because life is short and there's
a lot to see and do and enjoy and appreciate in the
few years we're here. So I think there's nothing
wrong and everything right with using part of that
money we've been loaned as stewards to enjoy
the heck out of the incredible world we've been
given.

The problem comes when access becomes
excess; when privilege becomes demand. Comfort and convenience can be seductive. After a
while, people can begin to think they *deserve*
these things and start to demand them as though
other people were less important or less worthy
or less valuable because they sat in coach or took
the subway or bought their clothes at an outlet,
or, horror of horrors, they are 16 and *don't have*

a car. And it's not a very far leap from there to thinking, eventually, that the rules don't apply to you the way they do to "lesser" people without your money and access – and therefore power. That's when the trouble starts at a whole bunch of levels. (Can you say, "Richard Nixon"?)

The funny thing about this is that, just like Tevya says in *Fiddler on the Roof*, we think people with money *know* more than other people. So the media ask them their opinion of world events, whether the man or woman is a sports figure with the IQ of a radish, or a zillionaire with the morals of a junkyard dog. Like it was *their* money anyway. As if!

The key here, as in so many things, is balance. To avoid thinking more of ourselves than we need to, it is important to humbly remember that it's not our own money, really. The money and I are just passing through here and when our paths cross we'll remember to amass, give and spend.

To avoid spending getting out of hand, some people "tithe." This is a biblical notion that says a certain percentage of your money should be given away – frequently 10 or 15 percent. If you got an allowance of $25 a week, you would donate from $2.50 to $3.75 of that to charity. If you made $50,000 a year, you would donate $5,000 to $7,500 to charity. For many people, this is a good way to keep track of how much they donate.

Another way to balance out what you donate with what you spend is to decide to donate the exact amount you spend on yourself for your own pleasure. If you spend $500 on a vacation, donate $500 to the Salvation Army. If you spend $200 on Christmas gifts for friends, donate that same amount to Meals on Wheels. If you buy three CDs for yourself, donate the equivalent amount to church or Hospice. It is a very powerful way to stay aware of the issue of stewardship.

You will hear it said that "Money is the root of all evil" and "Money can't buy happiness." Both are wrong. Money in itself is not evil nor the root cause of evil. When money becomes the symbol of power and authority it can corrupt, as you know Machiavelli said. But it also can be used for incredible good, as shown by philanthropists around the world. And anybody who thinks money can't buy happiness has never traveled with us. Of course it can buy happiness, and it should be used for joyous things. The "but" here is that the happiness is short-lived and of a different sort than the happiness of friendships, love, family, and giving.

A corollary to this is that everything has a cost, but not everything has a price. There are consequences to be paid for whatever we do, a trade off, a cost associated with each decision we make, and often that cost is monetary. For you to play varsity volleyball means that you will have to carefully manage your school and leisure schedules, arrange to get homework done before the weekend tournaments, stay up late many nights, lose sleep, give up trying out for the drama season, not babysit as much and lose income due to practices and games. There is a cost to playing volleyball. But when you win, or even when you play well and lose, the feeling is priceless. No amount of money in the world can buy the look on your face when you score an ace, or your team returns a difficult volley – or you go to state finals. So there are, in fact, many things money can't buy.

Finally, why am I spending so much time on this issue? Because I think you will have lots of money to deal with in your lifetime. I know that you and I both think this is the kind of problem to have, but it does come with its own burdens and dangers. Knowing you, I believe your values will help you balance out amassing, giving, and spending it. You are really good at taking care of what others entrust you with, whether it is the kids when babysitting, or the campers you supervise as a junior counselor, or your allowance for clothes and school, or Mom's car when you ask for it.

Because you are an excellent steward (I hesitate to use the word stewardess) of those things, I'd guess you will do the same with the dollars that God loans to you in your lifetime. So that at the end, you can stand before the king with that Michal-Meemer-slam-dunk-YES!-I-DID-IT! smile on your face and hand him your empty coffee can. Hopefully he'll grin and shake his kingly head and send you wherever I am so we can talk about it some more. With Mom. After hugs and smooches, of course.

nine

WHAT'S THE DEAL?

Obviously it wasn't the answer you wanted, though you knew from previous experience it was the answer you'd get. Could you go out Friday night with a group of girls, dinner at a local restaurant, back to the house of one of them to hang out, then home? My first response, since Mom was out at a meeting, was to say you'd have to call your friend back when Mom got home.

Although you wanted an instant response to what seemed to you to be a perfectly reasonable request, you already knew that in matters such as these Mom and I make no unilateral decisions. We always check with each other. In fact, this is to your benefit because Mom has less heartburn in some matters and I have less heartburn in others – so you actually stand a better chance with both of us than you do with one of us.

But you huffed off, telling the person on the phone your father said that for some silly reason he had to check with your mother. When Mom got home I asked you, "What's the deal?" Meaning specifically: Who's driving? Who's going? Whose house? Will parents be home? What time do you expect to be back? Though reluctant and annoyed, you dutifully asked the questions and came back with the answers and we said, "Fine. Sounds like a good time. Have fun." You left shaking your head.

This is my response to the incident and the headshake.

I remember being 15 and having to answer the same questions. I was embarrassed to have to go back and ask my friends for more information to pass along to my ridiculously over-protective parents. I was angry at them for the embarrassment and for not understanding that nothing could possibly happen that I couldn't handle entirely by myself. Or with Monty Steckler, my best friend who drove us everywhere. Fast.

But the issue here is inexperience. I wouldn't let you drive the car without driver's training and supervised experience behind the wheel because, after 33 years of driving, I *know* what the road is like. Likewise, each time you ask to do something (socially) you haven't done before, we as parents immediately evaluate the situation for 1. Safety, 2. Security, 3. Safety, and 4. Security. Why? Not because we don't trust you, but because we don't trust your inexperience and the inexperience of your friends and because we are terrified you'll end up hurt in some way.

The truth is Mom and I just have to learn to get used to it – but here's how that happens. *You* educate us about it. You teach us, through the experiences we have of letting go, that you are okay on your own. You've done it before. We've done it before together.

Mom held your hand (or you held her finger) while you put one stubby leg in front of the other and learned to walk. The more experience you got, the better you were at it, the less you grabbed for Mom and the more she let go. I held the back fender of your bike and ran with you as we took off the training wheels and you got experience steering and balancing. Eventually you taught me (showed me) you didn't need me to do that and I let go and watched you ride. Now you're 15 and we're doing the same routine only now it's with less tangible things like spending time with friends, and dating, and relationships, and thinking about college.

It is hard, as a parent, to let go of a hand or a fender or an emotional apron string partly because in some instances we *know* what lies ahead – falling on your diapered butt, or bonking your unprotected head, tipping over or running your bike into a stationary object, experiencing the consequences of your choices.

I have two basic rules for this: the Mike Wallace Rule and the Jean Rule. One is for me and the other for you.

There is an old joke that says you know it's going to be a bad day when you see Mike Wallace waiting to greet you at your office door. I don't want to be in a position where Mike Wallace asks me, "You didn't know where your daughter was going or with whom or who would be there or doing what?" And I have to answer, "Uh, no, it didn't occur to me because I obviously didn't care."

"What kind of irresponsible parent are you?" he asks.

"What are the categories?" I reply. "Can I pick more than one?"

Mike Wallace knows that parents are legally and socially responsible for you until you are 18 and that you presumably go places and do things under their supervision and knowledge – like walking and bike riding and car driving. He might also know that we feel protective and don't want you to get emotionally hurt even though we know it is inevitable as you let go of our hands and wave us off your fenders.

The second rule is about my former sister-in-law, Jean. When my first wife died very suddenly, her mother tried and tried to locate Jean, who was off with friends somewhere for the weekend. Jean was 19, had not left any numbers or names or places with her mother, and so didn't find out about her sister's death until she returned – two days after the funeral. She will live with that the rest of her life. That's why, when the three of us are separated for some reason, I am so particular about making sure you have a list of numbers and a way to get to us and vice versa. And that translates into my questions even about a night out with friends. I don't want any of us to end up like Jean.

Now there is a flip side to this and it is you. For the truth is that you always have been and continue to be an exceptionally responsible person. And you may have noticed (though admittedly it may be hard to tell in the heat of the moment) that Mom and I *have* let go more and more. Why? Because you have taught us that you are consistently responsible, and responsibility earns trust, and trust earns freedom – including freedom from the exhaustive questioning we now do. (Be assured there will *always* be questions due to the Jean Rule.)

Your actions, attitude, and behavior eventually teach us that you can and will take care of yourself on the way to the ultimate goal of more and more independence. Actually the *ultimate* goal is *inter*dependence, but that's another story.

So are we overprotective parents? Hell yes, we are. You and anybody else can accuse me of that any day and I'll be proud to admit it. It sure beats the alternative. And are you a great kid? Hell yes, you are. And we love you like crazy.

Now it may be that, after the questions are asked and reluctantly answered, we may still say "No" – in which case you will have to trust *us* to have good reasons that you may not understand or agree with, just as we trust *you* in many other situations to know better than we do about things.

On the other hand, as responsibility and trust grow, and as you continue on the road to independence that you have so successfully traveled so far, we will release your hand and fender and proudly cheer your success – tearfully, of course.

Finally, because we're your parents, our hands will continue to be available to hold you when you fall on your diaper or bonk your head or topple off your bike – and to help you stand up and go at it again.

Though we will still ask you, "What's the deal?"

ten

THE F-WORD

We just came back from running errands in the car and listening to your new CD of a comedy routine. Giggling nervously, you showed me the warning label on the front of the box stating "Strong Language and Sexual Material." To that you added your own warning: "Dad, you're not going to like this. Unless you really like the f-word." (I was hoping you meant "fart," but suspected that was too benign since we use it around the house so much – and it's always the *cat*, by the way.) Being the concerned, interested father that I am, I wanted to hear it with you anyway. Besides, I might miss something good.

So we listened. You broke me in on the piece where the guy goes to a psychologist to stop smoking. The counselor passes gas every five seconds, each louder and wetter than the one before. (Maybe that *was* the f-word.) Because I function basically at the junior-high humor level myself, I about drove the car off the road laughing with you. We had tears in our eyes it was so stupid and funny, especially when the counselor said, "Take a deep breath and relax."

The next cut where the *real* f-word appeared in abundance was not really funny, probably because it was sung and we missed half the words. The non-fucking ones.

The cow jokes with sound effects were creative and hilarious with neither f-word mentioned anywhere. We laughed without even knowing why, which made it even funnier.

But the last two cuts on the disc were over the edge for me, thus this letter.

The second-to-last was the one where he tapes people having sex and people working out and stops people on the street to see if they can tell which is which. Of course he only plays the ones of people having sex – including oral sex and anal sex – loudly, verbally, often with the word fuck liberally attending the various shouts and groans. Everybody guesses wrong (this is possibly funny but too predictable and repetitive) and he finally stops a woman on the street, tells her he's going to tape record something and see if she can tell what it is. He unzips her pants, tells her not to worry about anything, just relax; he gets excited too quickly and ejaculates. He plays back the tape, she gets it right, and he says, "Correct. Thanks for stopping by."

That, my dear Michal, is *pornographic*, sexist, and abusive. As a member of the female persuasion, if that doesn't infuriate you to the point of never listening to this guy again, you need to consider it further and be greatly offended. It is pornographic on two counts.

1. Tape recording anything, especially sex, between two consenting adults is not only illegal, it is unfair, like breaking into your private thoughts (or diary) and exposing them to the world on the front page of the McCallum High School newspaper, or the *Austin American States*person. Sex is something that is private, intimate, personal, and above all involves trust

and *vulnerability,* and any time anyone takes advantage of a vulnerable person they should be made to suffer some cruel and unusual punishment. (I have no strong feelings on this, as you can tell.) To tape record someone's private behavior is like stealing from them. It is a misuse of power and above all is just plain *unfair.* (You know I cannot tolerate unfairness.)

2. More importantly, the piece is pornographic because it graphically describes, makes fun and approves of, a man taking advantage of a woman for his own *use.* He is using her to obtain his own sexual feelings of pleasure. She is an *object.* This is not far from biblical times when women (until Jesus came along, anyway) were thought of as chattel, possessions like cattle to be traded, used, and bred. No one has the right to use another person for anything. That the comedian thinks this situation is a cause for humor means he thinks the woman is stupid or ignorant because she either doesn't *know* what she's getting in to, or worse, doesn't *mind* being used (since she knows her place is subservient to the man).

Now a quick word about pornography. It has nothing to do with naked people or f-words.

Nakedness is not pornographic, although you will hear some of our Fundamentalist friends proclaiming that very thing. To believe *that* is to believe that Michelangelo and Degas and Rodin are pornographic. Likewise words, in and of themselves, are not pornographic. But it is *how* the nakedness and words are used that *may* be pornographic.

When they serve to portray other people as objects to be used, they are pornography. War is pornographic. Concentration camps are pornographic. All misuse of *power* is pornographic. That's why sex crimes are crimes. They involve someone using their power (physical, political, social, parental, economic) to make someone else do something against their will. (Rape isn't about sex, it's about power.) That's why slavery was pornographic – people using people like unfeeling tools. And that's why seduction is pornographic (guys using girls or girls using guys). It is an untruthful, unfair, unequal balance of power in a relationship, like when the guy on the disc tells the woman to relax and not worry about anything. He doesn't care a damn about her, who she is, her feelings, her trust of him.

All he wants is to feel good at her expense. She might as well be an inanimate *Playboy* centerfold.

So in case I didn't make my point, that one was pornographic and I think the guy should have his testicles removed for including it on an otherwise really funny recording. Then we'd see how *he* feels about power games.

The last cut has him saying he's basically crazy and does "whatever he wants to do," like "whipping it out in a department store." This is pornographic because it is so incredibly selfish, self-centered and egotistical, like his penis is so important he can display it anywhere and any time he pleases, just because he wants to.

To a young mind feeling constrained by social and parental limits, "freedom to do whatever I want" sounds great. (It even sounds great to me.) But a very important thing to remember is that "freedom does not mean license." That's a biggie that I need to explain because the '60s generation thought freedom meant the *license* to do whatever they damn well pleased, whenever they damn well pleased. Many of the '60s kids thought it meant social, legal, sexual, and psychological *permission* to do anything, with no worry about the consequences of their actions to others or themselves.

Remember, whatever you do, that *there is no freedom without limits*. The guy may be free to wave his penis in public, but he does not have permission (license) to do so because we have decided as a society that certain things are against what we as a community believe to be decent, or commonsense, or private. Just as he is free to get a license to carry a gun, he is not free to wave it about in public whenever he pleases. He is free to speak his mind, but not to yell "FIRE!" in a crowded movie theater. In fact, we are only free to the extent that we *have* limits. People who have no internal or external limits are psychotic. They have to have others impose limits on them in the form of locked hospitals, straight jackets, or tranquilizing drugs.

A quick final comment about the f-word. Please remember I grew up in the German Meyer family where cussing was a part of everyday life, and then worked in a penitentiary where mother was half a word. The word does not offend me. The context might.

We have had other discussions about the incredibly satisfying feeling that comes from using certain words, but *only* in the correct phonic sequence! Sometimes a really emphatic "FUCK!" is required by the situation, like when something *really bad happens*. I myself reserve it for just such occasions and suggest you would do well to do the same. (That little incident where you backed the car into a pole and totaled the trunk comes to mind.) That's what bugs me about someone who uses it all the time. They're using up a perfectly good curse word and making it so everyday common that we'll have to come up with something else equally satisfying and there isn't one yet that quite does it like the f-word. Is nothing sacred anymore?

But the context that bothers me about fuck is when it is said in a violent, malevolent, angry tone, where, once again, power is being unfairly used – either physical power, as in rape; or emotional power, as in sex games like the one on the CD; or when guys try to make you feel guilty for not letting them use you as an object ("If you loved me, you'd let me."). You will find out later in life that employers and governments and religions try to do the same thing. Don't let them do it to you, either.

I will tell you a word that *does* offend me, though, and that is "retard." I know a lot of kids use it as a putdown or slam, and these kids have never walked through a home for the retarded, or known parents who had a retarded child. Any time kids use that word they are slamming other kids like the girl you visited with me in the hospital who had Down's syndrome. It's another misuse of power, like saying retarded kids are somehow inferior to you. Of *course* you're *better* at things than they are. Big "duh." Your arms and legs and brains work. But are you superior to them? A better person? 'Course not. Nobody has the right to judge that but God, thank goodness. People who have put themselves in that position usually end up starting wars and concentration camps.

Mom reminds me, and rightly so, that kids use the word "retard" to mean "slow" or "stupid," like butt-head, dumb butt, dumbo, dope. They're using a word they don't know the meaning of (like fuck in some cases). I get it. What worries me is that the word will be used in public next to a person who either *is* retarded or *has* a retarded person in their family. The word is right up there with "nigger" and other despicable epithets. I guess I've learned that the more familiar I am with someone or something, the less I am able to stereotype them or it. And I'm sure that's why kids use the word "retard", among others. I don't know. It bothers me when helpless people or animals are made fun of (with the possible exception of cats and politicians).

So anyway, thanks for letting me listen to the CD. I'm honored that you trusted me enough to risk playing it and I hope you know I trust your judgment in listening to it (where, when, and with whom). Basically I found it funny. More importantly, it was an occasion to raise other issues in my unending goal of getting you ready to leave the nest equipped with the emotional and intellectual ability to fend for yourself, which is basically all parents are for. Besides loving you, which I do.

Unfortunately, you are endowed with a sense of humor similar to your mother's and mine, which may limit your choice of boyfriends, but so what. Their loss.

Now can we go listen to that fart segment again?

Ffffffffffffffffffffffffffffft. Oops. Excuse me.

Actually it was you.

Or the cat.

eleven

BOOZE

You have just turned 17 and become a senior. Your big birthday present was Mom's car and your own cell phone to go with it. And a later curfew too. These things come at the end of a couple of years of yearning for wheels and earning more freedom with responsibility (and promptness about previous curfews), good grades (which gets you an insurance discount with State Farm), and excellent performance in athletics. These new ways of providing freedom and independence are quantum leaps forward, not just in technology but in unsupervised trust. So although we've chatted about it off and on over the years, it's probably time for the senior version of the booze-talk.

Since sophomore year you indicated that there would very likely be beer and liquor at parties. Though I'm sure you can hardly imagine it, I actually *was* in high school once, and it was not during Prohibition, so the thought of alcohol at parties had occurred to me. What had not occurred to me until recently (as you turned 17 and drove off in "your" car) was that it is entirely probable that you have had drinks at these parties, or while on overnights with friends. That may sound like a "big duh" to you, but you have never talked about it and I guess I just hadn't seen you as doing that yet. Parents are often somewhat slow on the uptake, imagining their little daughter's still in frilly pink dresses and white patent-leather shoes, somehow ignoring the jeans and Docs. Anyway, if you haven't yet imbibed at a party, given the fact that this will be your senior year, it is probable that you will do so in the coming months. So, given my desire to keep communication doors open and provide some modicum of rational thought (i.e., my un-

expurgated opinions) on how to approach the issue, I offer the following for your consideration.

You should drink in high school

Now, I know that teen drinking is a big problem.
I know the statistics on teens who drink to excess in high school in terms of grades, pregnancy,
dropping out, other drug use, driving fatalities,
and future potential for alcoholism. But adult
drinking is an even bigger problem. I also know
the statistics on adults who drink to excess in
terms of auto fatalities, domestic abuse, criminal
behavior, violence, and health problems leading
to earlier death. So any paternalistic and self-righ-
teous condemnation of drinking needs to be spread
wider than ages 12 to 20. Or as Jesus is well known
to have said, "Take the phone pole out of your own
eye before you attempt to take the speck out of
mine." Or something to that effect.

Alcohol is not going to suddenly vanish from
your life when we don't see you anymore and you
are off in college zillions of e-mail miles away. In
fact, if the descriptions of the colleges in the
Princeton and Fiske books are anywhere near

accurate, there is a distillery on every campus in the country and bumper stickers proclaiming "Beer – It's not just for breakfast anymore." So the problem with alcohol is *not* how to avoid it at all costs and feel guilty for drinking at parties, or happy because you got one over on adults who supposedly do not want you to drink. The problem is learning to handle a substance that will be at almost every party you ever go to when you come of age (if not before).

I *want you* to learn how to handle alcohol, or to begin the process, while still in high school, for a number of reasons. The first is that, hopefully, the glitz and forbidden attractiveness of it might wear off a bit with familiarity and you will be a little more desensitized to it. It might not be as big a deal in college and beyond if you've had drinks at home or with friends here. Second, we're here if you get into trouble. Learning what liquor does to your body and mind is usually a trial-and-error process, and a very effective one. Once you've had a hangover you know explicitly what *not* to do ever again and you swear to yourself you never will. But if you *did* get sick with alcohol poisoning, we would be nearby and be able to help, unlike once you are out of the nest. Third, your family can teach you a lot about alcohol that will save a lot of time and trouble, if you'll listen to the lore stored up in these wise old heads, especially those of Uncle Ben and Uncle Bud. The latter saved me lots of problems and I'd be happy to pass the info on to you, even though that probably takes some of the fun out of drinking behind our backs.

Actually, I think they should *teach* drinking in high school (would that make the name redundant?) as a sort of "Defensive Drinking Course" that educates young people on their choices, responsibilities, consequences, and alternatives. Kids would be required to learn the history of brewing and distilling, and taste every kind of liquor there is. They could learn about alcohol in other countries, reasons why people drink, what their own limits are and what happens when they exceed those limits, the cost to society, and the options for dealing with it. I'm sure that will happen the same day that the (Division-winning, going-to-the-State-Final Four) girl's volleyball program is allotted the same amount of scholarship money as the loud and losing football team.

It's illegal

One of the downsides for you is that possession of alcohol by a minor is a misdemeanor. If a neighbor calls the police and you are found with a container of any kind, you are subject to arrest, and the people who supplied the alcohol are subject to arrest for providing it – "contributing to the delinquency of a minor." The reasons for this, though you may disagree with them, are well thought out. Most kids, it is argued, don't have the maturity to handle alcohol and so will drink, hurt themselves or others, damage property, possibly kill someone, and become addicted for life. No one quite figures out how all these social-drinking adults learned to do it without any of those consequences, but that is the argument. The other reason is that, on this issue, we are a backward, unenlightened nation, unlike the French and Germans and Scandinavians and Dutch. (Are Belgians called Belch?) In Germany, you can drink at 16 but you can't drive till you're 18. Now *there* is a country that knows how to educate people according to their (no pun intended) motor skills. They give you time to learn to drink before you have to learn to drive.

You also need to know, if you don't already, that the consequences are pretty severe for falsifying an ID, which I doubt you would attempt, or even for being with someone who does. My fear as a teenager was that such a blemish on my record would follow me all through my employment career – which it would. Only it is worse now. When I was your age, inefficiently handled government and police records could get lost, or the clay tablets they were chiseled into would break or disintegrate. Now with computers if you fart the wrong way it follows you to your grave.

Until you are 21, possession and consumption of alcohol is illegal. So don't possess or consume it. Or don't get caught.

Zero, zero, zero

I do have one absolute titanium-clad rule for you at this level of your experience: *zero tolerance for drinking and driving*. Although you know I am usually reasonable on most items, I am absolute on this one. You are not to drink and drive. If there is alcohol at a party and you are driving, you are automatically the designated driver. This is not just another stupid parent thing (well, it may be that too, but it comes out of a sensible interest). The issue here is safety and inexperience. You are and will continue to be for a few more years, an inexperienced *driver* in an increasingly complex world of faster moving cars. Couple that with an inexperienced *drinker* who does not know the effects of different kinds of alcohol, the volume levels in the blood stream, how it affects what areas of the brain, and how and when it affects drowsiness and ability to judge distance – and you have death on wheels, or worse.

When you are more experienced (pick an age, say 46? – okay, realistically 24), you will learn that you can have a drink or two with dinner over a period of hours, metabolize the alcohol with the food, and drive just fine. Until then *zero tolerance* is the rule. If you violate it and I find out about it you lose all privileges for the car. Period. Responsibility is always rewarded. Parents should assume their kids will be responsible. But if the child (of whatever age) refuses to be responsible then it is in the job description of the parent to impose sanctions. The best way to keep parents off your case is to stay on your own case.

There is one disclaimer (isn't there always with me?) and that is that the *parachute* deal always applies. If you get into a situation where you cannot drive or do not want to drive, or do not want to get into a car with someone for whatever reason – use that cell phone and call me. Mom or I will be on the road immediately – *no questions asked*. And we will save the long instructive lecture till the morning.

Advantage

Unfortunately, as one of the female persuasion, you have to be particularly aware that you are especially vulnerable when under the influence of alcohol. In your normal state, you take no shit off boys and stand toe-to-toe and nose-to-nose with them in discussions, beliefs, and the issue of personal (body) rights and responsibilities. Alcohol can weaken, or appear to others to weaken, that incredible resolve you normally have. Guys, unfortunately, often use alcohol to do just that to women, and you may get taken advantage of, used, or possibly even abused. Your inexperienced smile may disagree, but why do you think they call it "date rape"? And why do the statistics show that most women knew their attacker? It is incredibly naive to believe that drinking doesn't open up the possibility of abuse or harm, even among friends (who also may have their inhibitions removed or relaxed under the same influence).

Again the issue is safety. I don't want to see you hurt. (Also you know we'd have to call Uncle Bud to "correct" the problem and plane fare from the coast is expensive.)

Reputation

If I'm really honest, I would have to say that my biggest deterrent to drinking in high school was the fear that when I got caught (not *if*) I'd get a police record and end up on the front page of the *Cincinnati Enquirer*. But things were easier then, I believe. At 18, in Ohio, we could legally buy 3.2 percent beer and pretend we were being mature big shits, smoking Mr. Steckler's imported Havana cigars and having a drink with him and Mrs. Steckler. But it is important to remember that, when you strip it all down, all you really have in life is your reputation, and that is built and maintained by your behavior. People who drink and drink to excess are thought of in one way and people who drink socially are thought of another way. Your choice. Just as every test you ever took from kindergarten to senior year ultimately builds on the others and counts toward college – so it is with which friends you choose and how you conduct your life and how you party. In my opinion, you've got great friends and you tend to attract good people around you (because of who *you* are), so this is not a big worry, though it is a consideration as you move forward to other places and other relationships. A good reference point before beginning something is to ask – How will this affect my reputation and how much does it matter, now and in the future? An even better one is to ask how it will make you feel about yourself, which is the even tougher reputation to live up to.

Drugs

I would be remiss if I didn't toss in other drug issues here, as they are parallel. Alcohol is (eventually, based on turning 21) a legal drug. You know I think marijuana should be legalized and sold in liquor stores, but that also will happen when your volleyball team receives as much scholarship money as the football team. (Perhaps if you started tackling the other team's players?) But the reality is that, unlike alcohol, when someone offers you an illegal drug, you have no idea what it is. In fact, you can be pretty sure it's *not* what the person offering it to you guarantees it is. I know this will come as a complete shock to you, but people who sell illegal substances often resort to lies and are not bound by the ethical dictates of the Better Business Bureau or the American Pharmaceutical Association.

Again, safety is the issue. I have related to you some of the stories I heard (and witnessed the consequences of) at the penitentiary where I worked. Inmates who bought drugs (often from long-time friends and dealers) at high dollar cost ended up with the high physical cost (brain or internal organ damage) of cocaine laced with rat poison, or marijuana soaked in strychnine. You know that my major reason for not doing drugs (other than alcohol) is my certain belief that I would be the one who got the "hot shot" and ended up drooling in my lap and giggling at everything while I pooped my Depends. Now we both know that that could happen anyway, but I see no reason to hasten the process or purposely bring on a stroke. Life is short enough as it is.

The legal consequences are much more severe than with alcohol, as these substances are *federally* illegal and the feds have no sense of humor about this issue (or anything else, for that matter). My bottom-line advice would be (can you guess?) to avoid these substances and the people who offer them like the ten billion gigavolt electronic fence around Jurassic Park.

Excuses

Although you are creative enough on your own and can make up excuses as quickly and convincingly as anyone, I thought I might offer some possibilities for those moments when a friend is suggesting you get drunk, binge-drink and throw up, drink and drive, or drink and get crazy, and you don't want to. (If you *do* want to, it may be a sign that the alcohol is being used for something other than a recreational relaxant, at which point it's time to talk to someone who will listen and help.) Here they are, not necessarily in order:

1. No thanks. I don't want it.

2. No thanks. I don't want it. And I'll hurt you if you try to force it on me.
3. My father will kill me.
4. My mother will kill you.
5. I will lose the car.
6. My 007 Uncle Bud will parachute out of nowhere and inflict pain upon your person in ways you cannot imagine unless you have seen a lot of old war movies.
7. My six-foot-five Uncle Ben will introduce you to the 12-foot reptile circling his stilt house in Florida.
8. Uncle Bud and Uncle Ben will inflict pain using the reptile.
9. If you were really a friend you would care as much about my brain as I do.

In fact, real friends *do* take no for an answer. Without excuses. Just because.

Trouble signs

In an airplane you know you're in trouble when the stewards and stewardesses are screaming up and down the aisles and the plane is spiraling downward. In a car you know it when you lose control of the steering or the brakes don't work.

Alcohol has similar warning signals.

At the first level, when your head feels a little light, you need to get some food down and cease drinking. At the second level, you might notice your coordination is affected – you trip or drop something. At the more severe level, if you close your eyes and the world is spinning (known as the "whirlies") you need to ingest volumes of water or vomit your stomach contents or both. The whirlies are a sign of poisoning and although you will probably live through it, it would be a good idea to have someone there with you while you do. What happens is that people lie down, go to sleep or go unconscious, vomit and aspirate the vomit into their lungs and choke to death.

If friends are commenting on your drinking it may be time to check and see if your personal brakes are out or you've lost control of your steering and loved ones are running up and down the aisle of your life warning you about a crash. Though society makes big fun of drunks and drinking, alcoholism is not a joke.

Let me quickly add that I do not expect that you will get to this level of trouble, or that you will *ever* become addicted or an alcoholic. Why? Because you hate loss of control and you hate being sick in any way, and you hate both being in pain and causing pain to others. These parts of your psyche and character are indelible and will enable you to be a social drinker, able to get along in society and drink the occasional drink and go on about your business. They may also enable you to decide you don't like alcohol or its effect on your body at all – and it's perfectly okay to say no to this offering just as it is to others.

Trust

The bottom line for me is this one – *trust*. I am not naive enough to expect you to tell me everything you're doing. I would be pleased and honored, as I always am, for you to feel comfortable enough to discuss drinking and sex as candidly as we do everything else in the sometimes late-night conversations that I so enjoy with you. I sometimes think that you think I will simply blow up or get angry and punish you severely for doing something with which I disagree – though I think you will note that that happens when you *don't* tell me and I find out some other way. Most of the time, if you've brought something to me that you've done wrong or where you know you screwed up big time, I may not like it and I may have a right to be angry about it, but when you act out of trust (and not manipulatively) we usually work it out, sometimes with you participating in setting your own consequence or punishment.

So while I don't expect to know everything, I do expect you to tell me if you have questions or concerns or problems you want to discuss as rationally as I am able. I am pretty good at listening to you nonjudgmentally, especially as you get older and more rational in your own thinking. That's what parents are for, to give you the benefit and warning of their own experiences. And then we'll helplessly stand by as we watch you choose your own path, just as we did with our parents' sage advice.

The important thing is for you to know that we'll love you if you don't drink and we'll love you if you do drink, and, just as with every other area of your life, we are willing to help you learn how to do it successfully so that *you* control *it* and not vice versa.

As the psalmist says, God created "wine to gladden the heart of humanity" (Psalm 104).

I'll drink to that. Maybe even with you, Meem.

twelve

CHURCH. PEW.

Going to church with you is always an adventure. When you were a little kid you would say outrageous things out loud. Once the priest said "Christ Jesus" and you corrected him. "That's backwards!" you yelled. Then there was the time we tried by *really* concentrating, to get the lady in front of us to itch her ear, after whispering that she had bigger ears than the lady in the stained-glass window beside us. But our all-time every time standard response comes during the post communion prayer where we are told we are "heirs through hope of the kingdom of God." Once in church you read it (extra loud to be sure I'd hear you) as "*hairs* through hope" and I blew snot out my nose laughing.

I am not certain that everyone else at the rather prim and proper 7:30 service appreciated the two of us sitting in the third pew from the front (so we could see), whispering back and forth and occasionally making noises that indicated we were either laughing or needing the Heimlich maneuver. At least we were never reprimanded by any of them, all of whom were old enough to be your great-grandparents. But I am certain this *is* the way to do church.

And God. Because God is far too important to be taken seriously.

Due to our rambling discussions over the years, you already know many of my religious prejudices, but probably not the depth of them, and I'd like you to know that before you launch out of adolescence. Also, because you are just beginning to get in touch with your own spirituality (though you might not define it that way) I feel compelled to offer a few – what shall I call them? – *reflections* on some of the issues your spirit will confront as it gets to know you better through the coming years of development.

God

Let's start with the biggie. In one sense I don't know where or who God is. On the other hand I know exactly where and who God is. That both of the preceding statements can be true is at the heart of spiritual reality. God is the ultimately knowable unknowable. The unknown known.

There are a lot of rationalizations about why we need to assume God exists. None of them work for me, or ever have worked for me, even as a kid. I don't *care* how the universe started or whether God invented the first subatomic particle and took a nap to let it all evolve from there. What I do know in my very bones and even deeper, in my soul, is that I am connected in a substantial way to every other thing in creation, animate and inanimate, and they are connected to me. And to you. And I believe that experience has something to do with spirituality.

I'm talking about a lot more than mere genetics or even the archetypal unconscious, though they are a part of it. Because, as my friend Keith Miller says, "the best descriptions are more about drama than doctrine," the best contemporary example I can think of is the trilogy you and I watched last summer – *Star Wars* – where what we call God is portrayed as "The Force." When you are in tune with the Force (or God), aligned with it, it empowers you, enables you to be fully who you are (alone and with others), and releases abilities in you that are only possible when you're connected to it – sort of like electricity or energy running through an appliance that is "off" until the current runs through it.

But unlike electricity or energy it is more than an "it," because it has both direction and purpose. The Force has *intention*. It moves always toward the Good, toward reconciliation, healing, mediation, community, and away from the dark side of disruption, hatred, brokenness, and fear. I believe that this intentional Force which we call God is in all of us, and in everything in the universe, connecting us and moving us toward becoming One with it – which is our true nature and when we are most free to be ourselves.

Religion

This is our way of acknowledging God as the Force and of trying to formally structure our response to and manage our relationship with it.

The word religion comes from the Latin words
re-ligio meaning "to bind again." It is our attempt
to bind ourselves to God again and again. It is where
we hear stories of how others before us tried to
do this and of how they succeeded and failed.
Those stories in our culture are in the Bible. They
are the stories of God's search for us and of our
reluctance to allow God in, to let ourselves become
one with the Force. In other cultures stories of
this same deep search, this hunger, this longing
for connection, are in the Koran, the Bhagavad-
Gita, the Upanishads and in other holy scriptures.
Most of these stories have the same point, and
many of the statements are even quite similar.
They all acknowledge our separation from what
we call God, and they all provide ways to "re-ligio"
us, to reconnect us, to bind us again to that which
is the essence of all life in the universe. Many paths
– same mountain. In the Bible I've found the story
that resonates with the deepest part of me, and
that also makes the most sense to me. And I believe with everything in me that the perennially
searching, inquisitive, seeking, childlike part of
you that I know and love so much will be drawn
toward finding the One that comes to you.

Jesus

If God is like the Force, the biblical Jesus is the human manifestation of that Force. We see in him what it can mean to be connected (bound again, re-ligio) with God and one way it can be lived out among other people.

Now I must tell you that even as a kid I never understood the theological stuff about how God sent Jesus to die for our sins as a sacrifice to atone for Adam and Eve's fall from grace in the Garden. To me that paints a pretty calculating and compulsive picture of a demanding God of wrath. Certainly one can make that argument from the literature. But here's another way to view it.

The entire Bible from Genesis to Revelation (and I know you can sing all the New Testament books) is the story of God's search for us, to re-bind or reconnect with us. It is the story of our rejection of God's outstretched hand because of selfishness, jealousy, feelings of unworthiness, or the belief that we do not need this unnecessary re-binding and are perfectly fine on our own without it. Over and over, God sends the early leaders – Abraham, Isaac, Ruth, Rebecca, Jacob, Leah, Deborah – prophets, judges, kings, rabbis, culminating in one last shot at it: Jesus.

Jesus' story is one of a gradual unfolding, of slowly discovering how truly bound he was with the focus of God, how much he was One with the Ultimate Force – how much he *was* it. It must have terrified him, given what he saw around him, knowing that humankind's history of rejecting the Force would ultimately mean rejection of him.

As people gathered around him they wanted him to do it all for them – to be the power of the Force for them so they wouldn't have to bind *themselves* to God. But he constantly turned the responsibility back onto them. When they brought people to him for healing, he told them to heal them themselves. When they asked him to feed the 5000, he told them to feed them themselves.

Ultimately, he became a threat to the political establishment and to the religious establishment. He was unsettling, revolutionary, even more radical in his belief than Obi Wan and Yoda, Buddha and Mohammed. Jesus saw the universe from a totally different perspective than the folks in charge, a perspective that confronted and frightened the keepers of the world's power and financial structures that selfishly maintained systems of wealth and poverty. He blew off their prejudices and the religious establishment's smug certainty about the nature of God and about their rituals being able to control the behavior of God. Instead of mere church attendance he wanted justice, equality, and above all, love. So because the world, the culture and the religious establishment felt threatened by him, Jesus had to die.

But his death, as in the stories of Obi Wan and Yoda, resulted in an incredible thing. Instead of killing Jesus, two things happened. The first was that the power and loving personal presence of the Force they had experienced in Jesus *exploded out* of him as Spirit, and *imploded into* everything and everyone permanently and indelibly – became accessible to everyone. So the power of God/Force expanded into the world in ways Jesus' enemies never imagined would happen, even into *them* (his enemies). The second thing was that the Force was so strong with Jesus that he returned to them – and the best word they had for what they experienced was "resurrection." What I think this means is that God/Force, seen in Jesus, keeps coming back at us, wanting to be known and to be loved and to be bound as one, reviving us, resurrecting us over and over and over again through every phase of our lives by clarifying every relationship, job, success and failure, love and hate, joy and sorrow, birth and death.

I believe that's basically what Jesus' life – and also the spirit he left in us – was all about: telling and showing us, and all who seek, that death and resurrection are what we do here repeatedly, with the help of God, along the path to becoming One.

Holy Spirit

If God is the Force and Jesus was the human manifestation of it, then Holy Spirit is the next attempt. It is as though God tried in the Old Testament to deal with us directly and didn't have much success at it. Then Jesus came along as one of us and we killed him, but in doing so multiplied the power of the Force immeasurably and unleashed the next incarnation of the Force, which is the Holy Spirit moving among us to help us re-ligio, to bind again, with it and with each other.

People today talk a lot about angels. You and I think we have had experiences with them. Remember the one by Mom's bed? Who knows? The Greek word for "angel" means merely "messenger" or one who is sent by God. In that sense the Holy Spirit is in all of us and there are many "messengers" who come to us at school and work, in family and friends, to do things to and with us that may lead us to re-bind.

The spirit is part of that circle of light we wrap around each other for safety when we part, an act of love and intention that binds us into the hands of the Force until we meet again.

Soul

If God is the Force, and Jesus is the Force in human form, and Holy Spirit is the current incarnation of it, then your soul is your individual manifestation of it, your piece of the One. It is the part of you that is fully the Force, seeking contact with the universal Force – to re-bind with it and be fully who you are.

Contrary to many people's beliefs this has nothing to do with being perfect or with always being right. It has to do with getting in touch with the part of you that is transcendent, that encompasses both your mind and your body and is more than the sum of both; the part that yearns for the One and that cautiously, tentatively reaches out to grasp the outstretched hand of God.

Your soul grows with you, but it also leads you, because it is in touch with that collective unconscious and the universal power of the Force. It is the part, I believe, that heals, comforts, cries, mourns, rejoices, and provides insight beyond intellectual ability. Your own soul, Meem, is wise beyond your years and has already guided you through difficult times. It will continue to do so, if you let it, and if you provide opportunities for nurturing it, for re-binding, recharging, and renewing it.

Church

I see the church as our best attempt, so far, at institutionalizing the Force and religion. The church has seen its mission as keeping the gospel story alive and as spreading it throughout the world. While a noble and even honorable intention, the downside is that we in the church have often been arrogant and bigoted, pushing its various interpretations of the truth as the *only* correct way of re-binding with God, and insisting that any other way is heretical or bad or wrong or threatening. As if the Force can't take care of itself with or without the church (or the mosque or the temple or the shrine).

At its best, the church has stood for the right against tyranny in Germany, South Africa, and the American South, and has diligently fought as the political and economic representative of the Force against racism, hatred, genocide, and apartheid. At its worst, it has been nothing but an empty God-box, demanding from us allegiance to outmoded concepts and refusing to keep up with a Force/God which is forever changing and evolving into the new.

Although I am not particularly fond of the "institutional church" as manifested in particular denominations, I do really like church buildings, especially in Europe. Even in our local church I like the smell of beeswax and musty stone. I love the stories told in the windows and appreciate the ritual and the words of the liturgy. All these things help me re-ligio, re-bind, and re-new with the One. They remind me, guide me, lead me in the right direction. That's why I go occasionally.

Ideally, people go weekly to remind themselves what is really important about life – the Force and its call to us. It is this re-minding through stories and liturgy that helps put the rest of what we do in the proper perspective, whether that is work, kids, school, relationships, money, misfortune, or even death.

This does not mean, as you have said, that I cannot find that same guidance elsewhere, and I do – in music, art, literature, nature. The Force is strong there as well. You will have to find where your spirit leads you and what resonates for you.

Prayer

This takes many forms, from conversational language to breathing and meditation. Mother Teresa and many Buddhists believe that right action is a form of prayer, as are good deeds (Hindu pujas and Jewish mitzvahs). I believe that the purpose of prayer is *presence* – not *outcome*. We pray to invite the Force into our life, our soul, our situation, to re-bind with it, to reconnect and be empowered. Somehow this makes a difference in what happens. As a result of prayer, people feel calmed, at peace, revived to go out and act for the good.

While I think it is important to state our desires and to say what we want to happen, that stating is more of an offering-up than a demand or plea for a payoff or a specific outcome. It is a conscious turning over of our desires and wishes to the Force, to align ourselves with whatever outcome we move toward with it, communicating in prayer every moment of the way.

Interestingly enough, you seemed to know this at an early age when the three of us used to kneel at your bedside to say our nightly prayers. You would do your "prayer flip" where you somersaulted out of bed and landed in a kneeling position by the side of the bed with your hands together. Then you'd pray for God to "help" us to do things, or to be safe or to help the animals in the cold and the homeless people sleeping under the Congress Avenue bridge. And that is exactly what prayer does – it invites the Force to "help" us by being with us and allows us to risk (have faith) that whatever happens, the Force is with us still.

Heaven

Every religion has this concept, Meem. Best I can tell, it is a way to describe what happens when our bodies die and our spirit/soul has yet another chance to re-bind with God/Force. If our soul decides to do it, to become One, to take the risk of not knowing what that will mean, what the outcome will be if it does, then it enters the state of Heaven. If not, if it chooses not to risk it and to stay apart, then my guess is it lives in eternal darkness and that is the best description I know of Hell. But always, throughout eternity, the Force is there tapping it on the shoulder, beckoning for it to re-bind, so that the option is forever present and all the soul has to do is turn around and be there in "heaven," welcomed into eternal light.

Sin

You hear a lot about sin being evil things that people do and for which they will be punished by horrific tortures such as the ones you read about in Dante's Inferno. In fact, the Greek word for sin is an archery term. It means "missing the mark" or not hitting the bull's eye. It suggests not being aligned (on target) with God, either aiming for it but missing or purposely rejecting the Force because we think we don't need it or are better than it, or because we don't believe in it.

Sin is more a state of being, or a condition, than an action or something we do. It's like feeling sad or depressed, or guilty or angry, or outcast or not quite yourself. That's why the Creed in church says Jesus "took away the *sin* of the world" – not *sins*. The suggestion here is that, although we have the Force in us, our human nature is an occasion for us to reject it and to rely on our human traits only, putting our faith in our human side only, rather than balancing out our human and spirit (Force) sides. When we do this we are out of balance, wobbly, and we "miss the mark."

Now you probably have already figured out that denying our human nature and thinking we are only spiritual beings is as dangerous and as much "sin" or missing the mark as denying our Force side. The goal here is to know both our human nature and our spiritual nature, to realize that they are inseparable, to accept them both, and to do our best to keep them balanced.

How do we do this? By doing our best to stay aligned with the Force. Paul (Apostle) said, "I am most free when I am most a slave to God." We are most fully human when we are most aligned with God or the Force.

Many people do this through prayer: through silent talking, meditative breathing, activities of doing for others, sacrificing their time and money for those less fortunate, or through fasting or going on retreat. Others go to a religious building or area and engage in rituals such as Communion or confession to experience forgiveness for the times when they have purposely aimed outside the bull's eye and have put human nature over spirit/Force, or vice versa.

I have come to believe that everyone has the same Force in them, and the same capability of connecting with the Force in others and in the universe, no matter how small that ability may seem to others. I think that's what Jesus meant when he said there is "neither Greek nor Jew, male nor female, slave nor free," but all have the same potential to relate to God.

Most importantly, the biblical story indicates that we are equally accepted and forgiven by God. Indeed, one of the ways of hitting the mark is by acknowledging our "sin" and wanting "forgiveness" (realignment), and by asking for it in prayer. That scenario is acted out in Communion and that's why people go. We start the service by acknowledging the Force as the power in the universe. We read stories of our interaction with it in the past to remind us of our relationship, of how we missed the mark and how we hit the mark. We symbolically *take* the Force in the form of the most basic elements – bread and wine; we *bless* these elements and bless ourselves as we admit our sin/missing and ask forgiveness/realignment; we *break* the bread and pour the wine to symbolize how it is now spread out into the whole universe, in everyone and everything; and we *give* it to one another symbolizing the fact that the Force is in us all equally again and we are now *one communion* or community with those elements inside us, restored to oneness with God. Finally we are *sent* out into the world to spread the Force and to align with it in others to "do justice, love mercy, and walk humbly," with God and one another.

This ritual mirrors what we do with each other, at least in our family. When we miss the mark with each other, one of us comes to the other, acknowledges our purposeful or inadvertent part in the event, and apologizes for that, asking forgiveness from the other – who acknowledges his or her part in it – and we *realign* with each other again, get back in sync, and go on until the next time. We're pretty good at it. Maybe because we've had so much practice.

Through many frustrations, failures, tears and confessions (some of which we have shared), I have come to be convinced that one of the most important things to retain in dealing with spiritual matters is a sense of humor. Like the time at the end of an interminably long prayer when everyone else said "Amen" and you said *"Whatever."* That is why I so enjoy going to church with you, or talking about these important subjects with you – because in the middle of something totally serious, one of us will burp or fart or think of something outrageously random or irrelevant and make the other one start laughing their brains out.

I think that's what God does with us as well. Just when we think we've got God down, that we understand the Force and the way God operates, love and new life break out somewhere totally different, in a different form than we ever imagined, to surprise us, scare us, and make us laugh at ourselves for ever thinking we could contain it in words or ideas.

As Obi Wan said to Luke, the Force is strong with you, Meem. If you let it happen, God will take you on a journey that will last a lifetime, to places in the world and in your soul that you never imagined were there; and will bring you, at the last, home with the rest of us who have gone on before, welcomed into oneness once again.

And all because we are "hairs through hope."

FURTHER READING

Other titles by the author

Meyer, Charles. *The "Saints of God" Murders*. New York: Berkley/Putnam Publishing Company, 1995.

———. *Blessed Are the Merciless*. New York: Berkley/Putnam Publishing Company, 1996. Stone Angel Books Reprint 1997.

———. *Beside the Still Waters*. Austin, Texas: Stone Angel Books, 1997.

———. *Surviving Death: A Practical Guide to Caring for the Dying and Bereaved*. Mystic, Connecticut: Twenty-Third Publications, 1988. (Second Edition, 1992).

————. *A Good Death: Challenges, Choices and Care Options*. Mystic, Connecticut: Twenty-Third Publications, 1998.

Meyer, Chuck. *God's Laughter: And Other Heresies*. Austin, Texas: Stone Angel Books, 1990.

————. *The Eighth Day: Letters, Poems and Parables*. Austin, Texas: Stone Angel Books, 1991.

————. *The Gospel According to Bubba*. Austin, Texas: Stone Angel Books, 1992.

————. *Fast, Funny, and Forty*. Austin, Texas: Stone Angel Books, 1994.

Bibliography

de Chardin, Teilhard. *The Phenomenon of Man*. New York: HarperCollins, 1980.

Niebuhr, Reinhold. *The Nature and Destiny of Man*. Vol. 1 and 2. New York: Charles Scribner's Sons, 1941.

Shedd, Charlie. *Letters to Karen: On Keeping Love in Marriage*. Nashville: Abingdon, 1993.

Weatherhead, Leslie. *The Will of God*. Nashville: Abingdon Cokesbury Books, 1944.

Wink, Walter. *The Bible in Human Transformation*. Philadelphia: Fortress Press, 1973.